Field Dressing
Small Game and Fowl

Field Dressing
Small Game
and Fowl

The illustrated guide

to dressing 20 birds and mammals

James E. Churchill

Stackpole Books

Published by
STACKPOLE BOOKS
Cameron and Kelker Streets
P.O. Box 1831
Harrisburg, Pa. 17105

Printed in the U.S.A.

Illustrations by Doug Pifer and Daron Fayas

Library of Congress Cataloging-in-Publication Data

Churchill, James E., 1934–
    Field dressing small game and fowl.

    1. Game and game-birds, Dressing of.   I. Title.
SK36.2.C48   1987   799.2'5   87-10010
ISBN 0-8117-2154-X

To Megan, Future Novelist

Small game

Fowl

PART ONE
SMALL GAME

The basics

Dressing wild game and skinning furbearers are old skills. The pioneers could skin a rabbit or peel the hide from a muskrat almost as fast as modern-day folks can remove the wrapping from a cut of frozen meat. But sportsmen can quickly acquire competence in this enterprise — and get the satisfaction that comes from having prepared their own catch for the table or fur buyer.

FURBEARING MAMMALS

For the hunter, mammals fall into two general classes, the furbearers prized for their skins, and the game animals taken primarily for meat. A few mammals, such as the raccoon, fit into both categories with their valuable pelts and edible meat.

Equipment

To get started, you'll need the right equipment. Specialized skinning and fleshing knives, fleshing beams, ready-made stretchers, and skinning gambrels are commercially manufactured and distributed by retail outlets and mail-order supply houses.

But it is not necessary to buy an assortment of special equipment to prepare fur skins for the market. Used with ingenuity, standard household items will suffice.

Skinning gambrel. Wire can be used instead of a skinning gambrel to suspend the animal. The animal should hang at a comfortable working height, with its hind legs splayed.

Knife. An ordinary pocket knife is adequate for making the necessary cuts in the skin, and for dismembering the carcass as well, if the meat is edible. Use a stone to keep it sharp.

Tailbone puller. The store-bought version is a convenience, not a necessity, since you can work the tailbone out of the skin with your

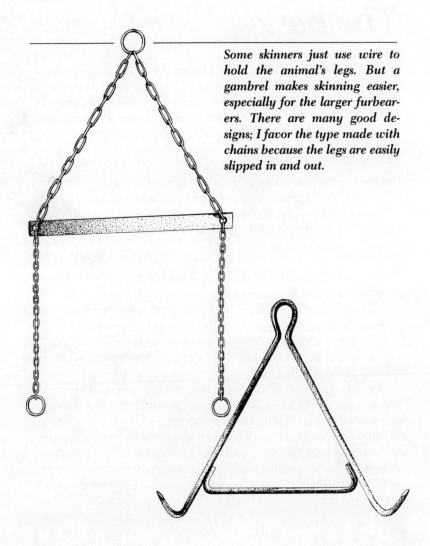

Some skinners just use wire to hold the animal's legs. But a gambrel makes skinning easier, especially for the larger furbearers. There are many good designs; I favor the type made with chains because the legs are easily slipped in and out.

fingers. But you can make your own tailbone puller at home, using a piece of milled lumber 4 by 1½ by 1½ inches. Saw it in half lengthwise. Clamp the two pieces back together in a vise, with the cut facing up. To accommodate tails of different sizes, drill one ⅝-inch hole and one ⅜-inch hole, centering the drill bits on the cut. (So that you don't misplace half the device, give it a quarter turn and drill a small hole near one end, then tie the halves together with a loop of stout line.) The device fits over the tailbone.

Fleshing knife. A dull butcher's knife can substitute for a fleshing knife. Drive the point of the blade into a piece of wood — about 1 by 2 by 3 inches — to make a second handle so that you can work the knife with both hands.

Fleshing beam. A temporary fleshing beam can be a pole 4 inches or more in diameter. Lean it against a bench so that the upper end is about waist height and the lower end abuts a wall or other stationary object to keep it from sliding away as you push on

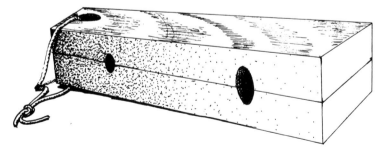

A tailbone puller, homemade or store-bought, will help. Fit the appropriately sized hole over the bone so that you have a handle to pull the tailbone out of its skin.

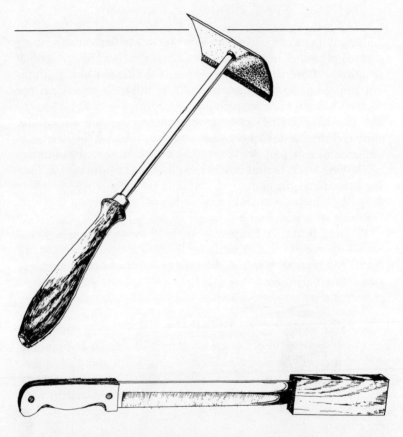

The two-handled fleshing knife (the one shown here is homemade) is for large animals. A one-handled knife is better for rabbits, squirrels, and muskrats but is also good for scraping around the eyes and legs of larger pelts.

the skin. The hide is slipped over the beam, skin side out.

Skin stretcher. Stretchers can be made at home from basswood or pine, either of which is soft enough to be easily sanded and to take pins yet not warp. Most trappers buy at least one stretcher for each kind of animal — from trappers' supply houses or rural hardware stores — and use them as patterns for making their own. Some hunters and trappers prefer wire stretchers to wood because they allow the hides to dry faster. But wooden stretchers are better for otters, whose large tails must be split and tacked open so that they dry flat. Use wood for foxes, coyotes, and raccoons as well if you want the pelts to have flat tails.

For beaver skins, you will need exterior-grade plywood at least ⅜ inch thick. A 4-by-8-foot sheet will accommodate four to six beaver skins.

Wedge. When wooden stretchers are used, a wooden wedge is usually placed between the belly skin and the stretcher. The purpose of the wedge is to provide enough slack that the dried hide will slip off the stretcher easily. The wedge should be about 1½ inches wide at the base and taper to a point at the tip. Make it as long as the pelt. After pulling the skin on the stretcher and pinning it, insert the wedge at the base of the belly skin and push it forward until the tip reaches the mouth. Pull it out before removing the dried skin from the stretcher. Some skinners use wedges with all types of skins, whenever they use wooden stretchers, but they are essential only for otters and coyotes.

Before you begin

All furbearing animals should be cleaned before they are skinned if the fur is bloody, dirty, or tangled. To remove burrs and sticks,

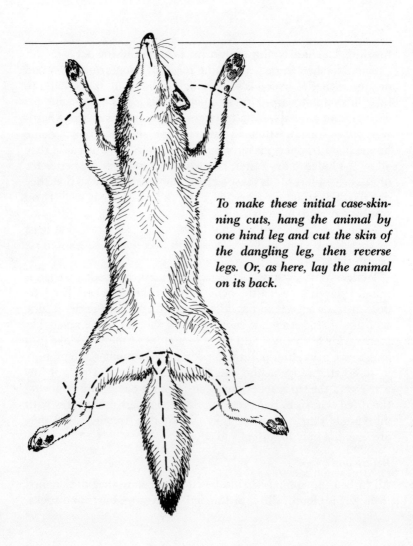

To make these initial case-skinning cuts, hang the animal by one hind leg and cut the skin of the dangling leg, then reverse legs. Or, as here, lay the animal on its back.

brush the fur with a heavy comb or steel brush. Mud and blood can usually be wiped off with a damp cloth. If the animal is exceptionally dirty, however, wash it in a tub of warm water containing a mild detergent. Then, so that the hide will not spoil, dry it promptly. Hang the animal outside where the wind can do the work. A faster way is to use a hair dryer after wiping the fur as dry as possible with cloths or paper towels. Do not put a fur too close to a source of heat, or it can be ruined. If you can't hold your hand in the heat, it is too hot for the fur.

Case skinning

Most furbearers are case skinned. You'll want to follow the specific instructions given in subsequent chapters, but the process is similar in each case. The hide is opened by slits in the skin on the backs of the hind legs. On most animals you insert the point of the knife under the skin at the hollow on the inside of the hock joint. Extend the cut to the crotch in front of the anus. Cut the skin on the opposite leg the same way. Cut a circle around the anus to connect the two cuts.

Except on otters, experts do not slit the tail skin to remove the tailbone. Instead, they work the bone out, using their fingers or a tailbone puller. But once the tail skin is free, it is slit and left open to dry, so it ultimately doesn't much matter if you have to slit the tail skin before the bone is out.

Use whatever works. The important thing is not to pull the tail off the hide.

After you have worked the skin loose from the legs and tail, pull it forward, inside out. Strip it off the carcass as if you were taking off a sweater.

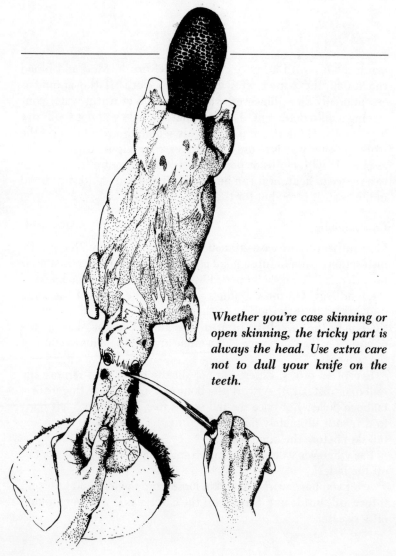

Whether you're case skinning or open skinning, the tricky part is always the head. Use extra care not to dull your knife on the teeth.

The skin should peel easily down to the front legs, where it will lock up. Work your thumb between the skin and the armpit to start peeling the skin down the leg. From the inside, cut the skin off at the joint above the foot.

The head skin is the last to be removed, and it is also the most difficult, since it lies tight to the skull. Usually, some tissue must be cut, but if you do it carefully, you will avoid making skinning cuts that mar the pelt. Further complicating the job are the ear and eye openings. The ears will appear as two white bubbles. Use the tip of the knife to cut the ear cartilage — and only the cartilage — right at the base. After the ears are free, pull the skin forward to the eyes, which will show as two dark bubbles. Again, use just the tip of the knife to cut the tissue around the eyes. Avoid enlarging the openings beyond their natural size. Finally, cut the cartilage on the inside of the nose to free the skin from the carcass.

The hide now resembles a tube. Next it is fleshed. Pull the hide, skin side out, over the fleshing beam and scrape the skin with a fleshing knife to remove all fat and meat.

When the hide has been thoroughly fleshed, pull it over an appropriately shaped fur stretcher to dry, still inside out. Center the skin so that the eye holes are on one side and secure it with nails or steel push pins. The skin is not really stretched on the form, just pulled tight and held in place so that it doesn't shrink as it dries. This step will prepare a skin to be tanned for a fur garment.

Open skinning

Beavers and a few other animals are open skinned. The hide is slit up the center of the belly and taken off in a blanket shape. An

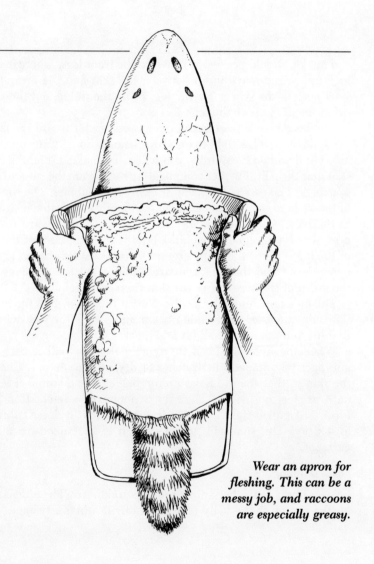

*Wear an apron for
fleshing. This can be a
messy job, and raccoons
are especially greasy.*

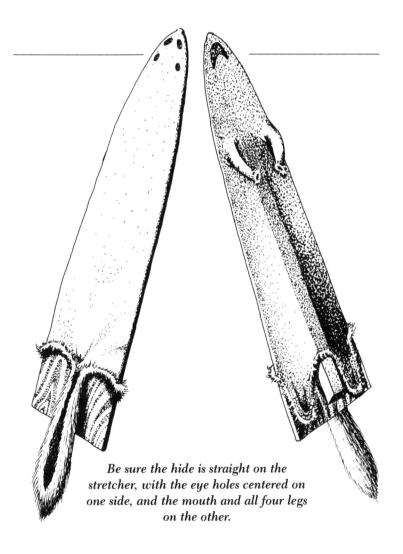

*Be sure the hide is straight on the
stretcher, with the eye holes centered on
one side, and the mouth and all four legs
on the other.*

open-skinned hide must also be fleshed to remove the fat and meat. It is then tacked to a plywood sheet or other flat surface to dry.

GAME ANIMALS

Squirrels, rabbits, and hares can be case skinned or open skinned if the hides will be kept for tanning. The skins are used for trimming gloves and other garments and for wall hangings. In most cases, however, these animals are hunted solely for their meat, and their skins are discarded, often in the field.

Skinning

The easiest way to take the skin from a small game mammal is to cut off the head, feet, and tail, then slit the skin across the center of the back, hook your fingers in the slit, and pull in opposite directions to tear the skin off in two pieces. More specialized methods are explained in the following chapters.

Animals that will be eaten should be skinned and eviscerated as soon as possible after they are killed. It is especially important to remove the guts quickly from an animal that has been shot through the body cavity, since the body fluids from the intestines will contaminate the meat and give it an off flavor.

Preparing the meat

The carcass can be cut into pieces or left intact for roasting. In either case, it should be thoroughly washed with cool water to remove blood and body fluids. All blood-shot meat should be cut out and discarded. Shotgun pellets in the meat can be found by probing the wounds with the tip of the knife. Be sure to remove all the pellets.

Small game animals should be allowed to cool for at least twenty-four hours before they are cooked and eaten. The meat should be cooled to 35 to 45 degrees F. — refrigerator temperature — if possible. Meat not cooked within forty-eight hours should be frozen. Wrap it in plastic, and then a double layer of freezer paper. Quick-freeze the meat.

Any meat that gives off an offensive odor when it is cooked should not be eaten. Rabbit and hare must be cooked thoroughly to kill any tularemia that might have infected the animal.

Beavers

Range. The beaver is found in Alaska, most of Canada, and all the contiguous states except Florida. In the many areas where the beaver population has recently increased, the animal is becoming a nuisance, cutting down valuable trees and building dams that flood roads and fields.

Size. The beaver is the largest rodent in North America. An adult is 3 to 4 feet long, including its 12- to 18-inch tail. Most adults weigh 45 pounds and up, attaining about 60 pounds after eight years. Since they continue growing throughout life, however, much heavier animals have been recorded, up to 110 pounds.

Pelage. Valuable fur covers the beaver's tubular, muscular body. The hair consists of coarse guard hairs and silky, dense, waterproof underfur. Most animals are brown, with a lighter belly, but some are almost black, and white beavers are occasionally seen. Both sexes are the same color.

The hairless, webbed hind feet have three straight middle claws; the outer claws curve toward the body. The second claw is cleft and is used as a comb for grooming. The front feet are smaller and unwebbed, with long digging claws.

The beaver's distinctive tail is broad and flat. Its muscular base is covered with hair, but the rest of the tail has black scales. The tail functions as a rudder for swimming, as a warning device — when the animal senses danger, it slaps the surface of the water — and as a prop to brace the animal for cutting a tree.

Habitat. The beaver is the only animal that creates its own environment. A mated pair or, occasionally, a lone beaver selects a site along a creek and builds a mud-and-stick dam that backs up the water. In the resulting pond the beavers build a lodge, also of mud and sticks. Inside are usually two levels, a lower room for feeding and an upper level for sleeping and resting. Here they remain safe from predators and keep warm during the winter.

Food. Beavers use the pond — and their strong swimming skills — to get around in search of food. They seldom venture far, however, usually felling trees at the water's edge. To cut a tree, they gnaw all around it, using their powerful jaws and long teeth. After it falls, they cut off the limbs and section the trunk into manageable pieces. They then float this food into the pond, where they can dine on the bark and small twigs. In fall, before ice covers their pond, they store a large supply of twigs, branches, and trunks near the lodge, underwater. When ice forms, the beavers must live on this store until spring.

Reproduction. Beavers are believed to mate for life. The breeding season begins in January and lasts until March. After a gestation period of 120 days, usually four or five kits are born. The newborn's eyes are open, it is fully furred, and it weighs about 1 pound. When three months old, it weighs about 6 pounds, and at nine months it reaches 12 to 14 pounds. Beavers stay with their mothers until they are sexually mature at two years of age. They then pair off and establish colonies of their own. Although they may stay close to their home range, young beavers have moved thirty miles before settling down. The lifespan is about twelve years.

Beaver

Properly treated, the beaver's pelt will be marketable and its flesh edible. Use the open-skinning technique.

Open skinning. Clean and dry the beaver and lay it on its back on a bench or other platform that enables you to sit or stand comfortably for skinning.

Cut off all four feet. They separate most easily where the fur and the bare skin meet.

Make a circle cut around the tail, but leave the tail on the body

Don't go too deep when making the belly cut on the beaver; the shallower the cut, the less fat will come off with the hide.

so that you can turn the beaver.

With the knife blade upward, slit the skin up the center of the belly from the tail to the lower lip.

Separate the skin by pulling it up at one side of the belly cut. Using the tip of the knife, make short, shallow strokes to "shave" the skin from the fat and flesh. The skin should be almost fat free when you have finished. Continue lifting the skin and cutting as you remove the hide until you reach the center of the back, then work the other side.

The skin will be tight on top of the head and around the ears, eyes, and nose. Following the directions given on page 19, pull the skin forward and cut it loose from the head. Cut the ear cartilage at the base and work the skin forward to the eyes. Cut the skin close to avoid enlarging the eye holes. Cut the nose cartilage, leaving the nose on the skin. The skin is now free from the carcass.

Place the skin on the fleshing

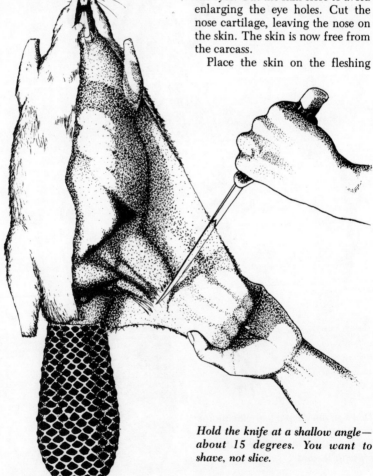

Hold the knife at a shallow angle— about 15 degrees. You want to shave, not slice.

beam and use a fleshing knife to remove all remaining fat and meat.

To stretch the skin, nail it hair side down to plywood or some other flat surface. Start by hanging the skin in a cross and then pull the skin, a little at a time, into a circle. Use 8d nails or staples to hold it in place. The hide may take a week or more to dry. When the ear cartilage is brittle, the rest of the hide is usually dry.

Beaver meat is edible—delicious to some. If the beaver was trapped in cold water and recovered within thirty-six hours, the meat will not have deteriorated. But an animal left in the trap longer than that should not be eaten.

Preparing the carcass. After the beaver is skinned, eviscerate the carcass, cut it into pieces, and roast it like beef or pork. The meat also makes good jerky. Be sure to remove all fat before cooking, since, not surprisingly, it tastes like tree bark. Beaver meat can be frozen for at least three months.

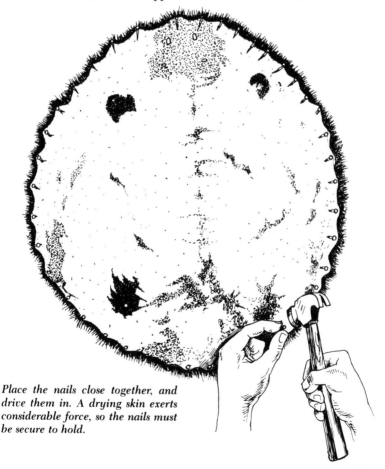

Place the nails close together, and drive them in. A drying skin exerts considerable force, so the nails must be secure to hold.

Coyotes

Range. The coyote is found in nearly all western and midwestern states. The animal has migrated east in recent years, and Maine, Vermont, New Hampshire, and some other eastern states now have resident populations of this little wolf.

Size. The coyote looks like a small shepherd dog — about 4 feet long, including a 12-inch tail, and about 2 feet high at the shoulder. Males are larger than females and average about 35 pounds, but a big individual might reach 70 pounds.

Pelage. The coat of a mature coyote is light gray sprinkled with black-tipped hairs. The muzzle and ears are reddish yellow, as are the outsides of the legs. The underparts are white or light gray. The animal's large, bushy tail is tipped with black. Because coyote fur is warm and does not frost up, as do some other furs, it is an excellent liner for hoods.

Behavior. Coyotes are good communicators. By howling, barking, whining, and using scent posts, they keep in almost constant touch with other coyotes in their territory. They are sociable and are usually found with their mates or other coyotes.

The coyote has strong legs and phenomenal endurance. It has keen eyesight, acute hearing, a superior sense of smell, and lightning-fast reactions. It is constantly alert and almost impossible to approach undetected.

Habitat. Coyotes are superbly equipped by nature to eat almost anything and survive almost any climate. They are found in the driest deserts, in the Far North where snow is a yard deep, and even in large cities.

Food. Coyotes are good hunters and opportunistic scavengers and can find food almost anywhere. In summer their diet includes snowshoe hare or cottontail rabbit and voles, ground squirrels, woodchucks, pocket gophers, muskrats, and porcupines. In spring young fawns and in winter deer floundering in deep snow may make up a large part of their diet.

Although coyotes prefer meat, they also eat berries, grain, fruit, fish, crayfish, mussels, and insects. Coyotes can even live on garden produce, and farmers in some irrigated areas in the West have considerable problems with coyotes that have acquired a taste for watermelon.

Because of the losses to farmers and ranchers, the coyote has been a target for more than a century, but with little success.

Reproduction. Coyotes mate in February, and the young are born about sixty-three days later, in April. A bitch has one litter a year, usually of five to seven pups. In four weeks the pups begin playing outside the den. At eight weeks they are weaned, and by August they are half-grown and more or less shifting for themselves. The family stays together well into autumn, sometimes all winter. The young animals breed the following spring.

Coyote

The coyote's size makes it somewhat hard to handle, and it is a difficult animal to skin, but the pelt is worth the effort. Skin the coyote while it is still warm if at all possible, since a warm skin is much more flexible and therefore easier to remove.

Case skinning. Hang the animal and make the customary case-skinning cuts.

The coyote's skin is tough to cut through and lies close to the body. Use the knife to cut tissue loose from the hide if it can't be pulled by hand.

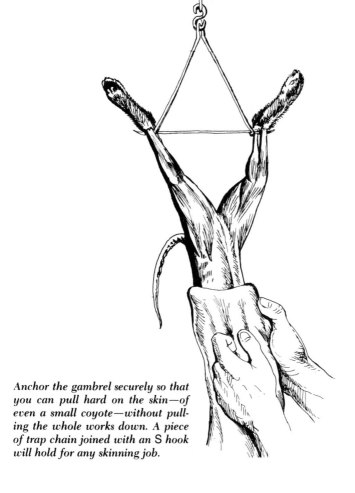

Anchor the gambrel securely so that you can pull hard on the skin—of even a small coyote—without pulling the whole works down. A piece of trap chain joined with an S hook will hold for any skinning job.

Make the customary cuts around the ears, eyes, and nose.

Pull the coyote skin on the stretcher, skin side out, and insert a wedge. Tack the tail open. Let the skin dry until it appears glazed, about a day in 30- to 50-degree weather. Take it off, turn it fur side out, and return it to the stretcher. The fur buyer can now examine the pelt and grade it.

Scent glands. These are a valuable product, used by individual hunters and commercial outfits for making lures and scents. The scent glands are two bluish pods, one on either side of the anus. Cut them out and keep them refrigerated or frozen until you can sell them or use them yourself.

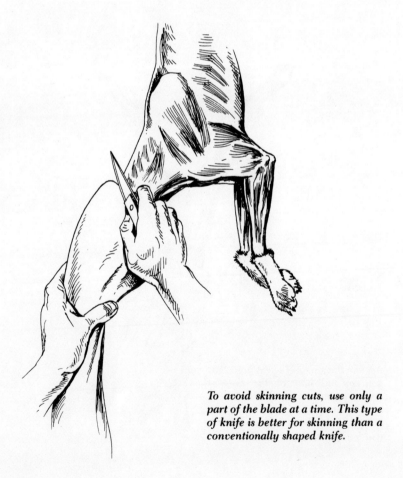

To avoid skinning cuts, use only a part of the blade at a time. This type of knife is better for skinning than a conventionally shaped knife.

Foxes
Red fox

Range. The red fox is found in nearly all the contiguous states, in southern Canada, and in southeastern Alaska.

Size. The red fox resembles a small collie, with large, erect ears. The adult is about 36 to 42 inches long, including a 13- to 15-inch tail, and stands about 16 inches tall at the shoulder. It weighs from 9 to 13 pounds, but heavier individuals have been recorded. Males are slightly larger than females.

Pelage. The tail is long and heavily furred and always has a white tip.

A conventionally colored red fox has a rusty or yellowish face and whitish cheeks, chin, and throat. The back is bright yellowish red with a dark line down the backbone. The rump is grizzled or light gray. The feet and the outsides of the legs are nearly black, as are the outsides of the ears.

There are genetic variants of the red fox, called color phases — black fox, silver fox, and cross fox — in which combinations of black hairs and silver-tipped black hairs replace the conventional red. There is no difference in color between the sexes.

Behavior. The red fox is territorial, and once it has picked out a location, it stays within a one- to three-mile radius unless forced out by danger or hunger. It is not gregarious and will fight other foxes that enter its territory. It is a mostly nocturnal animal but is active regardless of the weather or season.

Although its normal gait is a brisk walk, a fox can run 32 miles an hour. It dislikes getting its feet wet but will enter a river or lake and swim half a mile or more if necessary.

The fox is generally silent but can bark, yap, or scream. It has especially acute senses of sight, smell, and hearing.

Habitat. Nearly any environment is habitable, but the fox does best in hilly farmland of mixed woodlots, pastures, and cropland. It likes to be near water. Although usually found near people, it occasionally inhabits isolated locations, provided gray wolves and coyotes are absent and its food is plentiful.

Food. A red fox will eat almost any kind of animal or vegetable food, but its preference is for small mammals, which constitute about 75 percent of the diet. Rabbits and hares are the main staple, usually constituting about 60 percent of the diet, especially in winter.

Meadow mice, or voles, are the second most important food. The fox also kills a few deer — usually fawns and weak or crippled deer — and preys on birds, gophers, ground squirrels, tree squirrels, chipmunks, opossums, woodchucks, moles, and domestic animals, such as cats, lambs, and piglets. It also eats some fruits and berries.

The fox hunts by stealth, walking slowly with head up, keen eyes watching for prey. It usually stalks into the wind so that the prey doesn't smell it and, just as important, it can smell the prey. A mouse is pounced and held by the forepaws. A larger animal is seized in the mouth and killed by a bite at the base of the skull.

Foxes sometimes hunt in pairs, especially when chasing rabbits. One crouches beside a trail while the other courses through the rabbit thicket. Sooner or later a rabbit will hop down the trail toward the waiting fox.

Reproduction. Foxes may stay with the same mate for life. After the female is bred in late winter, between mid-January and mid-March, she cleans out an old skunk den or woodchuck hole for her nursery. The den is likely to be in open pasture, fence border, or open woodland — seldom in heavy cover. The burrow is usually 15 to 40 feet long. The young are born fifty-three days after the female is bred.

The young foxes are weaned at about two months. At first they eat regurgitated prey. Then their parents bring them dead but whole small animals to open and eat. When the parents bring them live but disabled animals, the pups must kill to eat. Finally, at about six months, the pups disperse to find territories of their own. Many young foxes starve to death, especially in places where food is scarce.

The normal lifespan in the wild is about ten years.

Fox

You must use great care when working on a fox, since skinning cuts will diminish the value of the pelt. Start by preparing the fur, which is long and thick and likely to be full of burrs, sticks, and dirt.

Case skinning. Comb out foreign matter with a steel comb, available from trappers' supply houses, and wash off mud and blood with soap and warm water. Dry the fur and hang the animal by the hind legs.

Make the initial case-skinning cuts across the hind legs.

Circle cut around the hock and

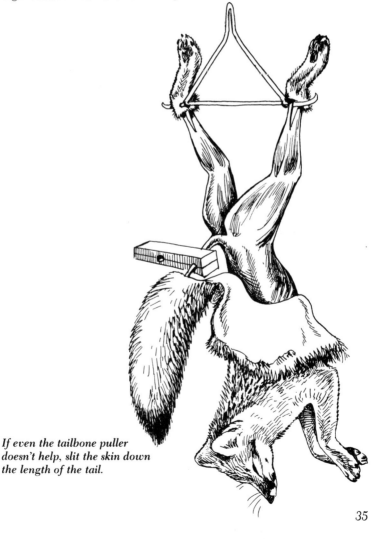

If even the tailbone puller doesn't help, slit the skin down the length of the tail.

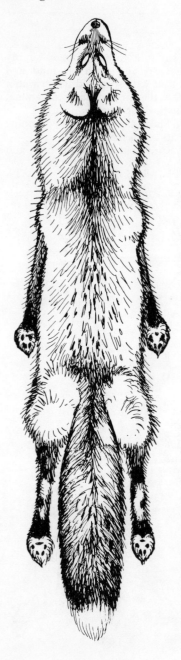

work the leg skin loose with your fingers, cutting tissue only when it can't be pulled by hand. Pull the tailbone out of the skin, using a commercial tailbone puller or working your fingers around the bone and peeling the skin inside out.

Continue pulling the skin to the front legs. Loosen the skin with your fingers and cut it from the inside by making a circle cut just above the feet. You can also leave the front paws on the hide, severing the paws at the ankle joint without cutting the skin. Most fur buyers do not care one way or the other, but if you are going to tan the skin yourself, the paws make a more interesting skin.

Pull the skin downward to the head and cut around the ears and eyes. Cut the nose from the inside. Use great care around the head: the knife is necessary to cut tissue, but be sure not to cut through the skin or enlarge the eye holes.

Pull the skin inside out over a fleshing beam and use a fleshing knife to remove fat and meat.

Dry the skin on a stretcher, skin side out, with a wedge. Tack open the tail. Allow the skin to dry for about twelve hours. When it has developed a thin, hard glaze, turn it hair side out and return it to the stretcher with the wedge. Let it dry completely—for a week or more.

For an intact fox pelt, like that shown here, skip the circle cuts around the paws. Instead, peel the skin down to the wrist or ankle joints and sever the tendons from inside.

Hares
Snowshoe

Range. The snowshoe hare inhabits remote and heavily wooded areas mostly north of a line stretching from central Minnesota to central New York but it also lives in mountainous regions as far south as California and North Carolina. These hares are common to abundant over most of their range. A typical density is one hare to five acres, but populations fluctuate on an eight- to eleven-year cycle, and in some years there may be one hare to every acre.

Size. The snowshoe is a medium-sized hare, smaller than the jackrabbit. It is about 15 to 20 inches long and has an average weight of 2 pounds, 14 ounces. The female is a little larger than the male.

Pelage. In the summer the snowshoe has a grayish brown pelage. There is considerable variation among individuals, and any given animal might have up to two dozen hair colors. About the first of October the animal begins its autumn molt. By December 1 the hare is almost completely white; only the tips of the ears remain black. About March 1 the hare molts again, and by May 1 it is grayish brown again.

The hare has a somewhat slender body and long hind legs. Its extremely large hind feet, with their winter growth of stiff hairs between the toes, help keep the animal from sinking in deep snow. Unlike the cottontail, which flounders in the snow, the snowshoe can run easily on the lightest powder.

The winter fur of the snowshoe hare is fragile but extremely warm. The Indians sewed strips of it together to make blankets for keeping warm on the coldest nights.

Behavior. Snowshoes escape their enemies by running. Unlike cottontails, they rarely retreat underground into burrows.

Habitat. The hare lives in brushy woodlands and heavy forest.

It is partial to a mixture of hardwoods and conifers, except in late winter, when it is usually found in cedar swamps or willow groves. The animal is seldom found in mature pine stands, which restrict light and thus limit the growth of ground cover.

Food. The snowshoe hare eats clover, strawberry ferns, and other green plants in summer, as well as the tender sprouts of hardwood trees and shrubs. In winter it eats woody plants, bark, and blackberry canes. When the snow covers its food plants, it retreats to swamps and feeds largely on cedar bark and needles. The hare will eat meat if it is available.

Snowshoe hare meat is edible, and early in the season it is as tasty as any rabbit. When the animal has been reduced to eating conifer needles and bark, the meat tastes stronger.

Reproduction. Hares mate in March. The leverets, usually three, are born in mid-April, after a gestation period of thirty-six days. The mother, or doe, births her young on the grass without making a nest, although she may use one of her resting places for the nursery. She may mate again the day her young are born, but although four litters a year are possible, most does have only two or three.

At birth the leverets are covered with fur. They begin to hop when they are a day old. At ten days they start to nibble grass, even though they continue to nurse for about four weeks. By five months they are mature, but they will not breed until the following spring. The snowshoe hare usually lives about four years in the wild but has a potential longevity of eight years.

Hare

The snowshoe hare should be fully dressed as soon after it is shot as possible, since it tends to develop an off flavor quickly.

Partial dressing. If you can't skin the animal right away, remove the entrails. Hold the hare in one hand by the center of the back, abdomen up. Insert the point of the knife at the junction of the rib cage and the belly and cut forward through the rib cage, opening it and exposing the lungs and heart. Then reverse the cut to open the belly and expose the intestines. The innards can be hooked out with a twig. Cut off the intestines at the anus. Wash the body cavity with snow.

Complete dressing. If you can, completely clean the animal in the field. Cut off the feet and head, then pinch the skin on the back and make a crosswise slit in the skin large enough to insert your index and middle fingers. Pull in opposite directions to tear the skin in two pieces and peel it off over the front and rear ends. If the belly skin is too tough to tear, cut it.

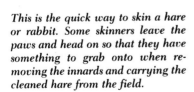

This is the quick way to skin a hare or rabbit. Some skinners leave the paws and head on so that they have something to grab onto when removing the innards and carrying the cleaned hare from the field.

Turn the carcass on its back and slit open the abdomen and chest, being careful not to cut too deeply and puncture the intestines. Continue the cut forward to the neck to open the carcass completely. Open the skin behind the anus and reproductive organs and remove the tailbone. The pelvic bone must be cut so that you can spread the hind legs and clean out the colon and urethra. Remove the intestines.

Wash the carcass with snow to remove any blood and body fluids.

If you hold the hare in a horizontal position, the innards tend to fall away from the meat and are less likely to be punctured when the belly is slit.

Preparing the carcass. At home, wash the carcass again in a solution of vinegar and water. The hare may be stuffed and roasted whole or disjointed into six pieces — legs, saddle, and rib cage. Clean the meat of all fat, which is strong tasting. For improved flavor, chill the meat to 35 degrees F. and age it for forty-eight hours. The meat will keep well if frozen.

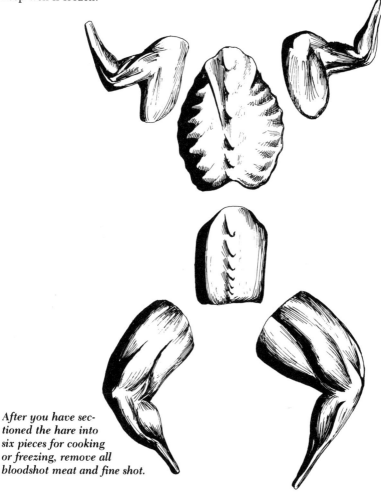

After you have sectioned the hare into six pieces for cooking or freezing, remove all bloodshot meat and fine shot.

Muskrats

Range. The muskrat lives anywhere in North America where there is enough sluggish water and vegetation to support its lifestyle. Muskrat populations are cyclic, varying from an average of one to fifty muskrats for every two acres of habitat. Muskrats are trapped for their fur and meat, and millions are caught each year.

Size. The muskrat's compact body measures about 24 inches, including a 10-inch tail. The tail, which is hairless and covered with scales, is flattened vertically, not round like a rat's tail. The feet are also hairless, and the hind feet are large and webbed for swimming. The muskrat's legs are short. The animal appears almost neckless, and the head is compact.

Pelage. The muskrat's soft brown underfur is overlaid with dark brown or black guard hairs. Generally, the animal is dark brown on the back, fading to light brown on the underparts.

Muskrat furnishes one of the most widely used furs. Probably more garments are made from muskrat skins than from any other animal. Muskrat pelts sold for 55 cents each in 1821 in Prairie du Chien, Wisconsin. Today, the pelts fetch about $8 apiece, and they remain an important trade item.

Behavior. The muskrats are prey to many predators, but they are far from helpless. They can dive under the water and swim about 3 miles an hour for 200 feet, holding their breath for 15 minutes. Muskrats are also fierce fighters and don't hesitate to defend themselves when they are threatened.

Habitat. In marshes, muskrats build domed houses from the roots and stalks of water plants. The houses are attached to a rooted plant or floating log or built on a bog. Muskrat houses are usually small, but with the additions built over several years, some measure 31 feet in circumference.

They also live in dens on the riverbanks. The dens are dug horizontally into the bank and sometimes extend 10 feet into the soil. In an above-water chamber the muskrats sleep and dine. Generally, muskrats that inhabit earth dens are larger and healthier than those living in floating houses.

From two to ten animals, usually family members, live together in a house or den.

Food. Muskrats live almost exclusively on green vegetation. Important foods include redtop grass, cattails, arrowhead, bullrushes, pondweed, and pickerelweed, plus the bark and leaves of willows and aspens. Muskrats are also carnivorous, however, eating mussels, snails, and crayfish when they can catch them, and old males sometimes become cannibalistic, killing and eating their own young.

Reproduction. Muskrats usually mate in April. A single pair of muskrats can produce two litters a year; the second mating usually occurs in August. In the southern parts of their range they may breed any month of the year and have as many as eight litters.

The average litter consists of eight young muskrats, born after a gestation period of about twenty-nine days. When the muskrats are two weeks old, they can swim and dive and begin to feed on vegetation. They stay with the mother until she has another litter.

Muskrat

Good pelts and a tasty supper—
these are what muskrats provide.

Case skinning. Clean and dry
the muskrat's fur.

Make the initial case-skinning
cuts across the hind legs and cut
around each hind leg at the hock.
With experience, you can skip this
circle cut and pull the skin loose
from the feet by hand. Work the
skin loose from the hind legs with
your fingers.

*I once watched a man skin a
muskrat in 15 seconds, using the
method given here. Start by making the cuts as shown.*

Work with your hands to loosen the hide from the belly, and slip your hands between the skin and the backbone. Now pull the loosened hide forward, pushing on the head to peel the hide to the front legs.

Work the front legs out of the skin and pull hard to loosen the

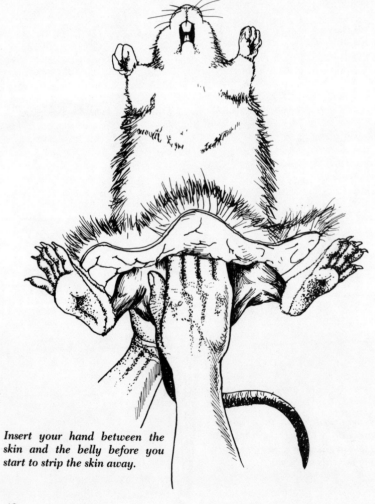

Insert your hand between the skin and the belly before you start to strip the skin away.

skin from the front feet. Or simply cut off the front feet.

Pull the skin forward to the head, cut the ear cartilage, cut the skin at the eye holes, and cut the nose cartilage on the inside, leaving the nose on the skin.

Pull the skin over a beam and use a fleshing knife to remove fat and flesh. Dry the hide on a stretcher, skin side out, with a wedge.

Preparing the carcass. Eviscerate the carcass after it is skinned. Wash away all blood and body fluids and roast the carcass whole or cut it into pieces for roasting or frying.

There are two ways to strip the skin off a muskrat: pull on the hind legs or push on the head.

Otters
River otter

Range. The river otter lives in northern North America, primarily near river systems and away from human populations. At present, otter populations seem to be stable and abundant.

Size. Otters have long, slender, muscular bodies. An adult is 3 to 4 feet long, including an 18-inch tail, and weighs 15 to 25 pounds. The male is about 5 percent larger than the female. The animal has a broad, flattened head, short legs, and large webbed feet with short claws. The tail is thick and tapered.

Pelage. The general coloration of a river otter is dark brown, but the belly is usually a shade lighter. Often the lips, chin, and throat are light gray. The soft, thick underfur is overlaid with long, silky guard hairs. There is no color difference between the sexes, but the older an otter gets, the darker its coat becomes; very old otters can have silver-tipped fur. The pelts are valuable to the fur trade.

Behavior. The otter is graceful in the water, swimming and diving effortlessly. It holds its front and hind legs close to the body and propels itself through the water with its body and tail. Its hind legs are also used for deep diving and surfacing. It can swim about 7 miles per hour. Although it can hold its breath for 2 minutes, it can stay under the ice even longer, snatching air from bubbles trapped beneath the ice. It can dive to 60 feet.

The otter has an unusual way of traveling across snow. It toboggans, tucking its front legs into the chest and propelling itself with the hind legs, and slides for long distances before losing momentum.

This is a restless animal. A mated pair or a lone male might establish a den but range out twenty to thirty miles, returning home after an absence of three weeks or more. At intervals an otter may seek a new home and travel a hundred miles or more to a new territory.

Habitat. Otters live an aquatic life and are always found near a network of rivers and streams or along the shores of a large lake. Although they are primarily a northern animal, they are also found in the Everglades and the Okefenokee Swamp.

Food. The otter lives almost exclusively on aquatic food. Crayfish make up a large part of the diet, but fish, clams, salamanders, and water beetles are also important food. The otter occasionally eats a young beaver, muskrat, or duck, and it will eat fresh carrion from a large animal, like a deer.

Whatever the meal, it swallows everything — scales, skin, bones, head — and vomits the indigestible parts.

Reproduction. Otters mate in spring, but because of delayed implantation the embryo doesn't grow until about two months before the young are born, usually in the following April. Three weeks after the pups are born, the female can breed again.

The newborns are covered with black fur. They are very dependent on the mother, who must feed them and guard against enemies. Such duties occupy all her time for about five weeks.

As nimble as the otter is when grown, it must be taught to swim. The mother introduces her pups to the water by giving them rides on her back. At about four months the young otters are able to hunt and travel, and they accompany the mother on her regular route.

Otter

This animal is a rare and beautiful trophy, but you need to dress it with great care. The skin lies close to the body and is hard to remove, and the large tail is difficult to skin.

Case skinning. Make sure the animal is dry and clean, then hang it up.

Make the customary skinning cuts across the hind legs and

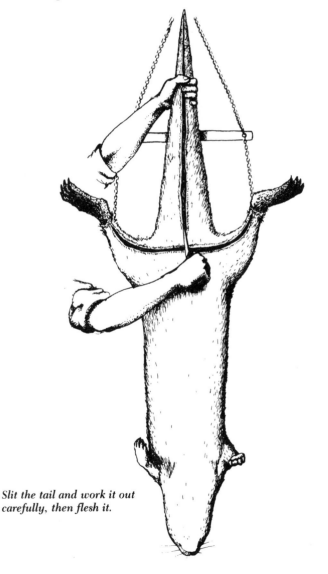

Slit the tail and work it out carefully, then flesh it.

around the hocks. Slit the tail skin on the underside from the base to the tip. Using the fingers and the tip of the knife, work the skin loose from the tail and hind legs. Otter skin is dense and tough, so take your time to prevent skinning cuts.

Pull the hide inside out over the body, using the knife to cut tissue only when you can't pull the hide by hand.

Pull the front legs out of the skin by working your thumb between the skin and the leg at the elbow. Cut the hide off at the joint directly above the foot.

Continue pulling the skin down to the head. Cut the ear cartilage and cut the eyes loose without enlarging the holes. Cut the nose cartilage from the inside.

Otters don't usually have much fat on their skins, but whatever is present must be removed. Be sure there are no burrs on the hide before you start fleshing, lest the fleshing knife make holes in the skin.

Stretch the skin inside out on a wooden stretcher, using a wedge, and tack the tail open. Let it dry.

Push your thumb between the meat and the skin in the armpit. Then pull the skin down over the leg to the foot joint and cut the hide from the inside.

Rabbits
Cottontail

Range. The cottontail rabbit is familiar quarry. It ranges from coast to coast and from southern Canada to South America. It is the only true rabbit found on this continent, and there are five major species: eastern cottontail, Rocky Mountain cottontail, swamp rabbit, cane cutter, and brush cutter.

Size. The eastern cottontail represents the approximate average size for all the cottontails. It averages 16 inches long and 3¼ pounds. The female is about 2 percent larger than the male. The eastern cottontail is smaller than the snowshoe hare; the cane cutter, largest of the species, is somewhat larger than the hare, even though it has shorter legs.

Pelage. The cottontail's distinctive white tail seems to bob as the animal bounds away. Its coloration is buff gray on the upper body with black hair tips. The nape and legs are cinnamon; the underparts are almost white. Unlike the snowshoe hare, this animal does not change color with the seasons, and there is no sexual variation in color.

Behavior. The cottontail is about at any time of day or night, but it is most active during the first three hours after sunrise and from two hours before sunset to an hour after. It can run about 18 miles an hour and maintain that speed for half a mile. To escape enemies, however, it depends more on dodging and ducking than on straightaway speed.

Habitat. Cottontails adapt to diverse habitats and are found anywhere from the deep woods to large cities, as long as they have good places to hide from their enemies — and since the cottontail is on the menu of most wild predators, the human hunter is not alone. Cottontails usually hide in a small clump of cover or in an underground den. An ideal habitat is sparse woodland with thick stands of sumac or elderberry patches, brush piles, and fallen trees. Average density is one or two animals per acre, but a cultivated hayfield or grainfield next to woodland will support many rabbits.

To find cottontails, examine the ground for rabbit feces, or pellets, wherever green vegetation grows and the snow doesn't get deep in winter. Once snow has fallen, rabbit tracks are easy to find.

Food. The cottontail is strictly a vegetarian, and in summer it eats well over a hundred different green plants. It prefers clover and alfalfa but seems to do just as well on wild grasses and weeds. It usually eats the youngest, tenderest plants, and garden plants like lettuce and peas are sure to be eaten if the rabbit finds them at the right stage. Where cultivated grasses and plants are scarce, the rabbit eats raspberry and blackberry twigs and shoots in addition to its diet of wild grasses.

In winter the cottontail eats grain or hay as well as bark and twigs from most smooth-barked shrubs and young trees — some seventy varieties. Sumac, aspen, and maple shoots are often heavily browsed.

Reproduction. Rabbits usually mate first in March. The gestation period is twenty-nine days, and the litter is born in April. A female rabbit usually has two or three litters a year, with three to six young in each.

The female makes a nest by scratching out a hollow about 5 inches in diameter and lines it with grass and fur plucked from her abdomen. At birth the cottontails are naked and blind and weigh only about an ounce apiece. She leaves them alone except to nurse them two or three times a day. When a cottontail is two weeks old, its eyes are open and it can play outside the nest and nibble grass. At four weeks it is weaned and independent. Most rabbits do not breed their first year.

The cottontail has an average lifespan in the wild of about two years.

Rabbit

If rabbit stew is your only object, skin the cottontail like a hare or squirrel—pinch up the back skin, cut crosswise, and then tear the skin apart. To get a hide ready for sale or tanning, however, skin the rabbit like a muskrat, then pull the hide over a muskrat stretcher.

But if you will do your own tan- ning, use the following method to obtain a skin that can be stretched flat and worked very easily.

Open skinning. Hang the animal up by the hind legs. Using a sharp knife, cut through the skin down the insides of the hind legs, the belly, and the insides of the front legs. Cut the head off.

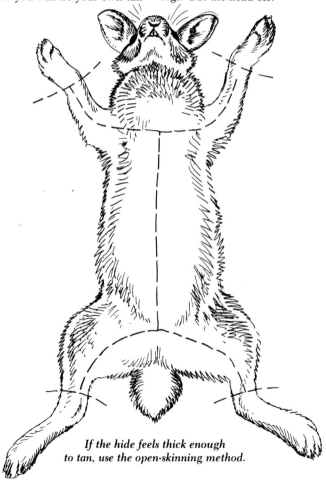

If the hide feels thick enough to tan, use the open-skinning method.

Use your fingers to peel the skin from the hind legs. Then grasp the two sections of skin and pull down to strip the skin off the carcass.

Flesh the skin if necessary, but be careful, since rabbit skin is very thin. Then tack the hide to a board to dry, skin side out. Pull and trim it into a rectangle.

Once the skin is loose from the hind legs, it can be stripped off the rest of the rabbit in one motion.

Preparing the carcass. With the carcass still hanging, slit the belly from neck to pelvis. Slip two fingertips inside to hold the intestines away from the belly meat while you cut. Split the pelvis to remove the colon and urethra tubes as well as the anus and reproductive organs. Take the animal down and cut the carcass into six pieces: legs, saddle, and rib cage.

When the rabbit is hanging, there will be a cavity under the belly flesh. Use your fingers to hold the intestines away from the knife.

Raccoons

Range. When the first Europeans came to North America, the raccoon was found only east of the Mississippi. But it has since expanded westward and is now found in all the contiguous states, most Canadian provinces, and Alaska.

Size. A raccoon usually weighs 12 to 20 pounds, but a few are much heavier, even up to 60 pounds. The animal measures 2 to 3 feet long and stands 8 to 12 inches high at the shoulder.

The raccoon has a husky body with a broad head and erect ears. Like a bear or human being, it has plantigrade hind feet. The front feet are dexterous and shaped like primate hands. All four feet have long, nonretractable claws.

Pelage. A raccoon is completely covered with valuable fur. Thick and soft with long guard hairs, it is prized for winter coats. The upper parts of the body usually have gray hair with light tips, but coloration varies greatly: some animals are nearly black, others are yellowish. The bushy tail has five to seven yellowish rings. The black face mask looks like the classic robber's disguise and gives the raccoon its nickname, the masked bandit.

Behavior. The raccoon travels slowly but can run about 12 miles an hour when it must escape an enemy. It is an agile climber and usually foils its enemies by climbing a tree. It is a fierce fighter, however, and can discourage a capable dog.

Raccoons seem to love water, especially shallow water for wading. Even though they are only fair swimmers, they take readily to deep water.

Raccoons utter several noises: a loud scream, which sounds somewhat like the cry of a screech owl; a harsh growl that signifies fear or irritation; and a soft purr for contentment. Low grunts, hisses, cries, and whimpers are also in the raccoon's vocabulary.

Habitat. The raccoon's favorite habitat is a forest of old hardwood trees containing many hollows, especially near a lake or river. But it does well in mixed farmland and forest and can thrive where cornfields predominate. It is also found in cities, denning in buildings or hollow shade trees and eating from garbage cans, gardens, and bird feeders.

Food. A raccoon eats nearly anything that has food value, but staples include all wild and domestic fruits, corn, acorns, and the tender buds and shoots of many trees and shrubs. When these foods are scarce, raccoons consume mostly animal matter — insects, snails, crayfish, fish, frogs, and turtles. They also eat birds, especially ducks; the occasional small mammal, such as a muskrat or squirrel; and sometimes carrion.

Reproduction. Raccoons mate in late winter, between the last week of January and the middle of March. They den usually in hollow trees but sometimes in caves or ground dens. The litter — four or five young — is born in late April or May, after a gestation of sixty-three days.

The young raccoons weigh 3 ounces at birth but reach 3 or 4 pounds at ten or twelve weeks, when they are weaned. They stay with the mother at least until autumn; some remain until the next spring. During this time she teaches her young to avoid enemies and find food. The family hunts together during the summer and early fall, but the young start hunting on their own as they mature.

A female raccoon mates when it is a year old. Life expectancy is five to six years in the wild.

Raccoon

The raccoon is an easy animal to skin because its thick layer of subcutaneous fat makes the skin somewhat loose before you even begin work. Nevertheless, many skinning cuts can occur on the head, and you must be careful with the knife.

Case skinning. Wash and dry the animal, and hang it by the hind legs.

After making the initial case-skinning cuts, work the skin loose around the hind legs and at the base of the tail, using your fingers.

Pull the tailbone out of its skin, using a tailbone puller or grasping the skin in one hand and the bone in the other and pulling in opposite directions. Take care not to tear the

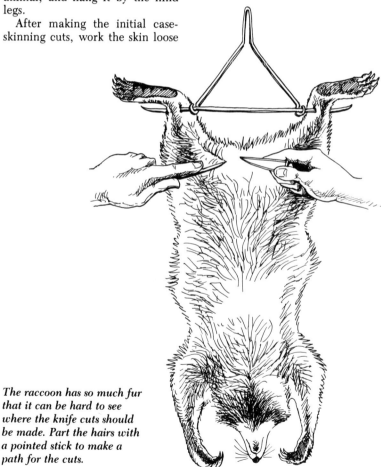

The raccoon has so much fur that it can be hard to see where the knife cuts should be made. Part the hairs with a pointed stick to make a path for the cuts.

tail. If the skin doesn't pull off the bone easily, slit it on the underside, from base to tip. When the tail skin is free, open it out so that it will dry.

Pull the skin down over the raccoon's body. To avoid skinning cuts, don't use the knife any more than necessary.

Working the skin with the fingers, pull the front legs from the skin and cut the skin at the last joint.

Cut the skin at the ears and eyes and cut the nose cartilage at the inside.

Preserving the hide. Because some fur buyers prefer to flesh and stretch the hides they handle, you may preserve the skin until it's time to sell by turning it hair side out, wrapping it in plastic, and freezing it; let it thaw before the fur buyer inspects it.

To flesh the skin yourself, stretch the hide over a fleshing beam and scrape the fat away. Fleshing takes only a few minutes because raccoon fat comes off easily—an experienced skinner can do the job in less than five minutes—but be careful not to press too hard and cut the skin. The fat and skin can be distinguished if you look closely; when you have finished, only the white skin should show.

Pull the skin over a stretcher, skin side out, and leave it to dry.

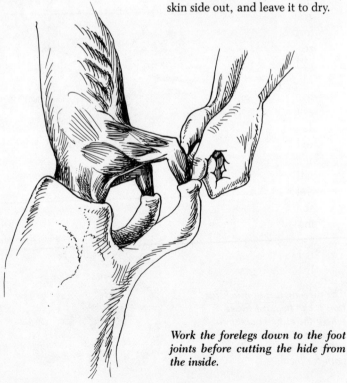

Work the forelegs down to the foot joints before cutting the hide from the inside.

Squirrels

Range. Squirrels are a favorite quarry of hunters in North America. There are many species, but it is convenient to consider three categories of diurnal tree squirrels: gray squirrel, fox squirrel, and red squirrel.

The gray squirrel is found primarily in the oak forests of the East, Midwest, and South, from Canada to the Gulf Coast. The fox squirrel has a smaller range, which lies roughly in the center of the gray squirrel's. Red squirrels inhabit all of North America's coniferous forests, especially in the north.

Size. The gray squirrel commonly weighs 16 to 28 ounces and is 18 to 21 inches long, including the 8- to 9-inch tail. The fox squirrel is larger, 20 to 22 inches long and weighing 24 to 32 ounces, sometimes more. The red squirrel is the smallest, about 11 to 13 inches long.

Pelage. The gray squirrel has a small streak of white or brown on the belly. The tail is used for balancing and warmth.

The fox squirrel is orange on the belly. The back and sides are typically duller. In the Southeast a nearly black form of the fox squirrel is common.

The red squirrel is rusty brown, with gray or white underparts.

Behavior. The gray squirrel can leap 5 feet, run 20 miles an hour, and climb an 80-foot tree in less than 20 seconds. By flattening its body, it can sail to the ground from almost any height. It is nearly always active, except during heavy rains and snows and extreme heat or cold.

Although it, too, can sail through the air, the fox squirrel doesn't leap about in trees as much as the gray squirrel, and it often escapes its predators by running.

The red squirrel is the most active, out almost every day, all day long. It escapes its enemies by jumping from tree to tree or disappearing into a hole under tree roots.

Habitat. Gray squirrels depend on oak trees that bear good crops of acorns, and most animals are found in hardwood forests, usually two animals per acre. When gray squirrels overpopulate their range and exhaust the food supplies, they disperse, swimming rivers and crossing highways in their search for new territory.

The fox squirrel prefers open woodlands and fringe areas. It has a low tolerance for other squirrels and rarely overpopulates its range. The animal is usually found in pairs or alone, occupying about two acres.

The red squirrel lives in coniferous or mixed coniferous-deciduous forests. There are usually about three squirrels per acre. They customarily stay within 500 feet of their dens or nests.

Food. Although acorns are a squirrel's staple, it eats nearly every nut, seed, and fruit. The animal also gnaws the inner bark of trees, especially in the spring, and eats mushrooms, insects, and if available, meat.

The provident gray squirrel stores food for winter, burying several hundred acorns and other nuts in an inch or two of soil. In winter it wanders about, sniffing the ground until it finds a nut to dig up.

The fox squirrel also stores food for the winter, but it can live for a week without feeding if the weather keeps it housebound. It is selective about its feeding times, often emerging only on sunny days and then only in early morning and early afternoon.

In addition to the usual squirrel diet, the red squirrel eats the seeds of pinecones. It, too, stores food for winter, harvesting the cones before the seeds ripen and fall out and squirreling away a bushel or more in a hollow log or stump.

Reproduction. All squirrels have two litters every year. A gray squirrel builds its nest from leaves or dens in a hollow tree. There are two to four young per litter.

An adult fox squirrel can build a strong, weathertight nest from a half-bushel of twigs and leaves in about 25 minutes. It also dens in hollow trees.

Red squirrels construct nests of twigs, leaves, and pine needles, usually in conifers but sometimes in hollow trees and earth dens. They may have two to seven young; four is average.

Squirrel

Good-tasting meat is your reward for expert handling of the animal after it is shot. Unless the weather is very cold, skin and gut the animal immediately — within a few minutes of shooting it. The sooner you skin the squirrel, the easier it will skin.

Skinning. Clean the fur, cut off the head, tail, and feet, and lay the squirrel on its belly. Pinch the skin in the middle of the back and cut across the back. Insert the forefinger and middle finger of each hand under the skin and pull the skin in half, in opposite directions, toward the front and toward the rear.

This simple method may not work for an older, tough squirrel, and you may have to work the legs

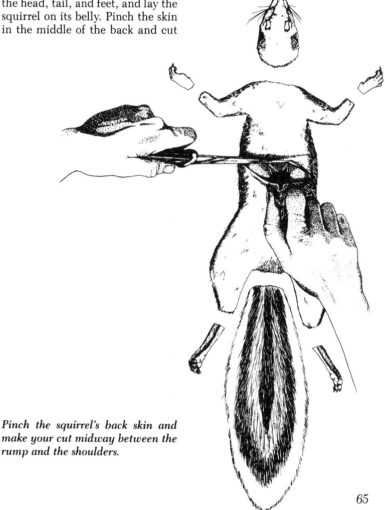

Pinch the squirrel's back skin and make your cut midway between the rump and the shoulders.

out of the skin, one at a time. Grasp each leg at the end and push it back into the skin as if you were turning a glove inside out.

If the skin does not tear into two sections, cut the strip of skin under the belly. The genitals and anus must be cut off under the skin before the skin will come free.

Preparing the carcass. Clean off the hair from the carcass.

Slide the point of the knife just under the flesh of the belly. Don't cut too deeply or you may open the intestines. Slide the knife forward, cutting belly tissue and opening the rib cage. Open the crotch by carefully slicing through the pelvis. The anus and urogenital tubes should be worked loose from their attachment in the upper pelvis. Remove the intestines by hooking your forefinger under them and lifting them out. Use the knife only when necessary to cut tissue holding the intestines.

Reserve the heart and liver; both are edible.

Wash the body cavity with cold water to remove all blood and impurities. The squirrel carcass may be roasted whole or cut into six serving pieces: the four legs, the saddle, and the rib cage. Cook it within a few hours or freeze it. To avoid freezer burn, double wrap the meat or freeze it in a plastic milk carton full of water.

As you slip the knife under the belly skin, be careful not to cut too deeply and nick the intestines.

PART TWO
FOWL

The basics

Game birds are somewhat easier to get ready for the table than mammals. The only difficult step is removing the feathers — and turkeys and waterfowl, with their thick feathers, can be difficult to handle. But there are three ways to do it: dry picking and singeing, wet picking, and skinning. Then the carcass can be eviscerated and disjointed. Parts of the bird may be needed for identification, so check applicable game laws.

Equipment

Most of the equipment for picking, eviscerating, and disjointing birds is already in the household.

Knife. An ordinary folding pocket knife, if kept sharp, is adequate for field eviscerating and can even be used for scraping off feathers and disjointing the bird. But a butcher's knife with a flexible blade or a filleting knife will do a better job of deboning and filleting out the breast meat. A heavy butcher's knife is good for cutting out the backbone and scraping when you are wet picking. Special game bird knives with gut hooks are available from hunting supply stores.

Game shears. Use these to quickly shear the ribs and remove the legs, the neck and wing feathers, and the wing tips. Heavy household scissors or tin snips can be used instead.

Containers. A five-gallon pail is big enough for wet picking the birds described in this book, but a larger container will be slightly more convenient for dipping turkeys and geese. You'll also need a basin to wash the cleaned birds.

Thermometer. An ordinary cooking thermometer is adequate for monitoring the temperature of water for wet picking.

Paraffin. This is the type of wax used for canning food. Twelve cakes will last most hunters a year, since much of the wax can be recovered and reused.

Propane torch. This is used for singeing feathers left after the bird has been picked. If a torch isn't at hand, ignite a rolled-up newspaper.

Some hunters pull as many feathers as will come out easily while they are in the field so that the bird cools quickly, then finish the job at home.

Pliers or tweezers. These are used to extract feathers that won't come out any other way.

Rope. Have a 3-foot length of rope or wire to hang the birds for picking and dressing.

Plastic bags. Take some plastic bags or empty bread wrappers with you to the field so that you can protect defeathered birds.

Cooler. A cooler is needed when the weather is warm — and it's convenient anytime — to keep the birds from spoiling.

Fish-filleting gloves. Worn when dry or wet picking, they provide a better grip and keep the hands warm.

Dry picking

Grasp the bird by the feet or neck with one hand and pull the feathers out with the other. Pull in the same direction as the feathers lie, both to make the job a little easier and to avoid tearing the skin. Feathers that are short and hard to grasp can be pulled somewhat more easily if you roll them between the thumb and forefinger. Pluck extremely short or stubborn feathers with tweezers or pliers.

Singeing

After a bird has been dry picked, any remaining feathers may have to be singed. Depending on the age of the bird, singeing may be necessary after wet picking as well. Young birds and birds in the initial stages of molt often have hairlike pinfeathers growing under their developed feathers. These pinfeathers will not come out, so you must burn them off. Pass the bird through the flames from a propane torch or burning rolled-up newspaper. For safety's sake, do this outside.

Wet picking

Birds are wet picked when their feathers are too difficult to pull by dry picking. First, dry pick as many feathers as will come out easily. Then fill a container — it should be large enough to hold the bird, with considerable overrun — at least half full with water

Be careful when dipping a bird in hot water and wax. The liquid can cause a bad burn.

heated to about 180 degrees F. Hold the bird by the head or feet and dip it in the water several times. Try pulling the feathers each time you lift the bird. When ready to pick, the feathers will slip out with little effort. Pull the feathers rapidly, since they set up as the skin cools. Dip the bird again when the feathers won't pull out.

Waterfowl are picked more easily if wax is added to the scalding water. Drop in a cake or two of paraffin; it will melt and rise to the top. As you dip the bird, the wax will coat the feathers. Let the bird cool so that the wax hardens and seizes the feathers. Then scrape with a dull knife, working toward the head; the feathers will come off with the wax.

Wait until the wax has hardened before you start to scrape. Use upward strokes. The feathers will come off with the wax.

Skinning

It is easier to skin some birds than to pick them. Usually, the skin can just be torn off, but some birds have tough, close-lying skin that must be opened with a knife. Make a slit up the breast and use pliers or your fingers to strip off the skin and its feathers.

Eviscerating

If you didn't gut the bird in the field, do so after the feathers have been removed and the head and feet cut off. I eviscerate birds as soon as possible, always within four hours of bagging them.

Slit the skin between the vent and the point of the breastbone and remove the intestines through the opening. Excise the vent after the viscera have been removed to avoid puncturing the guts. Reach forward into the body cavity and take out the heart and lungs. The lungs spoil quickly and may contaminate the meat.

The giblets—heart, liver, and gizzard—are edible after they have been prepared. Slit the heart so that any blood clots can be cut out, remove the green bag of bile from the liver, and open the gizzard to remove the food and grit it contains. Also take out the white lining from the inside of the gizzard.

At the front of the breastbone is the crop, a transparent sac that holds undigested food. Slit the skin on the lower neck and remove the crop and the windpipe, to which it is attached.

Remove the preen gland, an oil sac on the top side of the tail bulb. This gland contains the oil that birds use to coat their feathers, and it can cause off flavors in the meat. Also probe shot holes in the bird with the point of the knife to find the pellets.

Using cool water and vinegar, wash the edible organs and the entire carcass of the bird, inside and out.

Aging

Although some hunters hang their game birds until parts of them turn green, I don't believe any flesh should be aged to that extent. I age birds for twenty-four to forty-eight hours at 35 to 45 degrees F. If they are not to be cooked within that time, I freeze them.

Birds can be frozen in the feathers, which will keep them from drying out. If they are plucked before being frozen, wrap them in a layer of plastic wrap and two layers of freezer paper. Keep the freezer at about 0 degrees F.

Dabblers
Mallard

Range. The mallard is the most abundant and widely distributed duck in the Northern Hemisphere. It is found from the subtropics to the Arctic in North America, Europe, and Asia. There are some 6.35 million mallards in the United States and Canada.

Like most ducks, mallards are migratory. They have a more extensive breeding range than any other duck — almost all of the northern third of the United States, northwest to the Bering Sea. But the most preferred regions are the southern parts of Saskatchewan, Alberta, and Manitoba. Some mallards also nest in the southern United States.

Size. The adult male mallard averages 2 feet in length — the female is about an inch shorter — and weighs about 2¾ pounds. It is a stocky bird, with a short tail and broad wings that are set far back on its body.

Plumage. Even in flight, the green head, brown chest, violet blue speculum, and white outer tail feathers clearly identify the drake. He has a yellow or greenish yellow bill and coral legs and feet. The hen is straw colored with dark brown streaks and a violet blue path on the wings; her legs and feet are yellow, and her bill is orange splotched with black.

Food. Mallards have a varied diet. In the Far North they feed primarily on bullrush and pondweed seeds, but in the southern part of their range they eat smartweed, millet weed, and acorns. Other important wild foods are wild rice, cut-grass, beaked sedge, reed, canary grass, spike rush, burr seeds, and the leaves and stems of aquatic plants.

Mallards also eat cultivated plants — corn, wheat, barley, peas, rice, sorghum, and soybeans. In saltwater coastal areas, aquatic animals form an important part of the diet.

On dry land the mallard feeds by pushing its bill along the ground, opening and closing it rapidly. In water the same motion is known as dabbling, and since mallards get most of their food underwater, they are often called dabbling ducks.

Reproduction. Mallards usually start to pair off in late summer, until by January about 90 percent are paired. The rest do not find a mate until they have returned to their breeding grounds in the spring. The ducks usually migrate north in large flocks and separate into pairs upon reaching their destination.

Each pair selects a territory for the nesting site — a small pond or a section of a larger wetland area — and defends it against other ducks. It is the drake that usually chases the intruders away, producing the effect of two drakes courting one hen.

Once the territory has been selected, hen and drake fly low looking for a nesting site. They show great indecision, sometimes shopping for days. They usually nest on upland territory within 100 yards of water. Many locate on dry shoreline or dams only a few feet from water, however, and some nest as far from the water as five miles.

The female makes a bowl-shaped depression in vegetation or moist earth. She lines it with vegetation scraps and starts laying her eggs — an average of nine — about three days later. During her laying period she spends about an hour a day at the nest and then flies out to her mate, who waits at a predetermined site. When the clutch is complete, she stays on or near the nest; usually, the drake abandons her and shortly begins his summer molt.

Incubation takes twenty-six to twenty-eight days. Once hatched, the ducklings rapidly lose their down. They have feathers at six weeks and can fly at two months. About this time the hen starts her molt, and the family group breaks up. A mallard's lifespan is about eight years.

Mallard

Mallards are among the best-tasting of all wild ducks, and this makes them very good fare indeed. To preserve their good flavor, attend to the birds quickly.

Warm weather. Pluck the bird right away — it will pluck most easily when it is still warm — or if that is not practical, pluck the breast feathers so that the flesh cools quickly.

Next, eviscerate the bird by making a horizontal cut under the breast and pulling the innards out; reserve the giblets. Wipe out the body cavity, but unless clean water is at hand, do not wash it out. Remove the crop and windpipe.

Keep the duck in the cooler until you can refrigerate it.

Cold weather. In cold temperatures duck hunters need not remove the feathers or innards immediately. In several hours the carcass will have cooled and the feathers set. Remove them by a combination of dry and wet picking, followed by wet picking with wax.

After the duck is plucked, cut off the head and feet and remove the guts. Since the bird was not eviscerated immediately, the giblets will not be safe to eat and should be discarded.

Preparing the carcass. The carcass can be sectioned before cooking or roasted whole. You can also partially cook it, strip the meat off the bones, and then press the meat together to make salmi.

A mallard can also be boned completely before it is cooked; follow the directions for boning the bluebill.

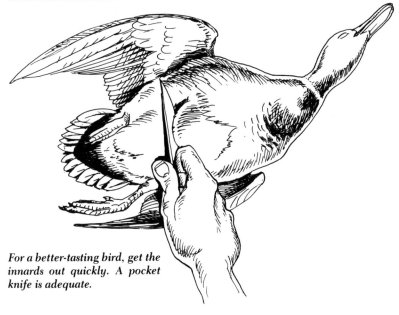

For a better-tasting bird, get the innards out quickly. A pocket knife is adequate.

Divers
Bluebill

Range. Numbering nearly seven million, bluebills, or lesser scaups, are the most abundant diving duck in western North America. They are found from Minnesota to northeastern California, and as far north as the Bering Sea. Drakes outnumber hens by about three to one.

Size. The male is about 17 inches long and weighs slightly less than 2 pounds. The female is a bit smaller.

Plumage. The drake's black head shows a purplish cast. Back feathers are light gray with wavy lines, or vermiculations, of sooty black. Lines on the sides and flanks are narrower and lighter. The drake's breast and upper belly are white, and the lower belly is sooty black.

The hen's head, neck, and chest are reddish brown; the back rump and scapulars are dark brown. Her white facial patch usually changes to light brown in the fall.

In both sexes the bill and feet are blue gray, the eyes are yellow, and the tail is black.

Food. Bluebills feed by diving. The water may be as shallow as 1 foot or as deep as 45 feet — deeper than for most other diving ducks — but is most commonly 10 to 25 feet deep.

They feed primarily on animal life, eating clams, snails, midge larvae, dragonflies, damselflies, nymphs, leeches, crabs, and small fish. But in some areas they also feed heavily on plant seeds and leaves, such as water lily seeds, pondweeds, widgeon grass, smartweed, wild cherry, wild rice, and bullrush. The mix depends primarily on what foods are available.

Reproduction. The bluebill does not usually breed until its second year. Bluebills begin to pair off on their winter grounds in December. By migration time in late March and April, most have paired off; the rest apparently find mates en route to the nesting grounds.

The hen selects the nest site in grassy areas near a shoreline, usually accompanied by her mate and sometimes by a second drake as well. If she does not find anything suitable, they may fly to upland areas, as far as 900 feet from water. A favorite place for a bluebill nest is a mat of floating vegetation, but they also nest on islands and in upland grainfields and hayfields.

The nest is shallow, built up with plant stems as the eggs are laid, and without much down. The hen lays about nine eggs. She meets her mate each day at a resting site while she is laying, but when she starts to incubate the eggs, she neglects the rendezvous, and he usually leaves the area in about ten days.

The ducklings hatch in twenty-four days. The female stays with them until they are about four weeks old — still in the downy stage — and then abandons them. Abandoned broods often combine, and sometimes one hen may escort three or four broods of downy ducklings by herself. The young bluebills take flight when they are about forty-seven days old.

Adult drakes fly into staging areas for their annual wing molt. Most reach the molting areas by July 1. The hens join them after they abandon their broods. Two big molting areas are the Athabasca and Saskatchewan deltas in Canada, where tens of thousands of bluebills congregate. By September the birds can fly again.

Bluebill

The bluebill is a good eating duck, but because diving ducks have small legs and wings, some hunters just fillet out the breast and discard the rest. Others bone the entire carcass. Both methods make it easier to trim away fat, which may impart a fishy taste. And to my palate, the meat tastes better once all the bones have been removed.

Filleting. First pull the breast feathers or skin the breast so that the body structure is visible. Find the keel bone that divides the breast. Slice on each side of it, using a boning knife or a fish-filleting knife, and separate the two halves of the breast from the bone.

Even if you fillet out only the breast, very little meat goes to waste because the rest of the bluebill is mostly bones. Scavengers will utilize the carcass.

Boning. First pluck the bird by wet picking. Then lay the cleaned bird on its breast and use a boning knife to slice on each side of the backbone. Slice through the flesh and cartilage so that you can peel back the opening.

Continue skinning the flesh away from the skeleton. Separate the wing joints and leg joints from the rest of the skeleton at the ball joints; you may need a heavier knife for this. Now the rest of the skeleton can be cut loose from the meat and lifted out, leaving only the leg and wing bones still in the flesh.

Remove these bones by cutting the flesh free with the tip of the knife.

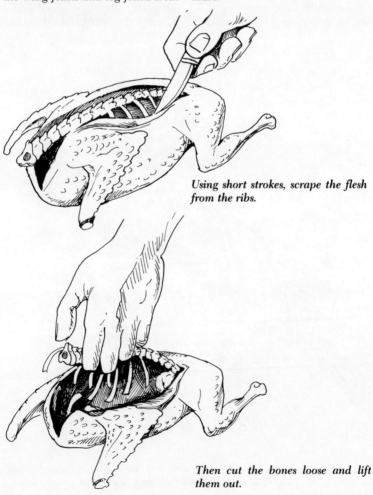

Using short strokes, scrape the flesh from the ribs.

Then cut the bones loose and lift them out.

Geese
Canada

Range. There are eleven subspecies of Canada geese, one or another of which is found all over the United States, Canada, and even along the western Gulf Coast of Mexico. Populations are at an all-time high. As many as two hundred thousand geese stage in the Horicon Goose Refuge in Wisconsin when they are migrating south in the fall. There are probably three million Canada geese in North America today.

Size. Subspecies of the Canada goose vary considerably in size and weight, from the diminutive cackling goose, whose wingspread is about 45 inches and top weight about 3½ pounds, to the giant Canada goose, which has a wingspread of 68 inches and can weigh 12½ pounds.

Plumage. The Canada goose is hard to mistake for any other bird. It has a black head and neck with a white cheek patch covering the throat. The back and wings are dark brown; the sides and breast are lighter. The belly and flank are white, as is the under tail, but the upper tail and rump are black. The bill, legs, and feet are also black. There is no difference in coloration between the sexes or among age groups.

Food. Canada geese have benefited greatly from agricultural crops, both along their migration routes and in their wintering grounds. This has been a major factor in the recent high populations of the bird, and there are probably more Canada geese today than when the Pilgrims landed at Plymouth Rock.

Corn, oats, buckwheat, and soybeans are their favorite cultivated grains. Among the wild plants in their diet are roots, stems, and marshes of spike rush, the American bullrush, wild millet, and wild grasses. Geese also browse on greenery — clover, barley, wheat, alfalfa.

Reproduction. Canada geese pair off when they return to their summer range in the north. Pairing occurs within hours among older geese that have lost their mates, but young geese may require weeks to form an attachment.

The pairs remain together for life, but if one bird dies, the other will mate again.

Both mated and unattached geese return to their summer range in flocks, but the pairs break away after they have reached the nesting grounds to lay claim to nesting sites, which they defend by aggressive calls and displays. The gander often flies up to challenge intruders.

Canada geese nest in marshes, on islands, on muskrat houses, on elevated platforms in trees and on cliffs, even on haystacks. Abandoned heron and osprey nests and rocks in the middle of rivers also make good sites. All nests are close to water and are hidden or camouflaged yet allow the female a clear view so that she can watch for enemies.

The female hollows out a depression about 6 inches deep and 2 feet in diameter, which she lines with vegetation and with down plucked from her breast. She continues to add down to the nest as she lays eggs.

The Canada goose usually lays five or six dull, cream-colored eggs. The goose incubates them while the gander keeps watch a short distance away. She leaves the nest in early morning and late afternoon to preen, bathe, and feed; he accompanies her and stands guard. The eggs hatch in about twenty-six to twenty-eight days.

Both parents escort the young away from the nest as they go about finding food. The female broods the goslings at night and frequently throughout the day for the first week and at night for several more weeks. The gander defends the family against intrusion by other geese, but where goose populations are dense, family groups may join together; gaggles of a hundred goslings and twenty-one adults have been observed. The goslings can fly about sixty days after hatching, but the larger the subspecies, the longer it takes.

Adult geese start to molt about three weeks after their young have hatched and don't regain their ability to fly until the young are ready to try their wings.

Canada

A wild goose, especially a large Canada, is a formidable creature to divest of its feathers. It has large flight feathers, an outer layer of contour feathers, and an inner layer of down. These must be removed, since they retain body heat and cause spoilage.

Dressing. Eviscerate the goose soon after shooting it.

To remove the feathers, dry pick or wet pick or skin the bird.

Skinning is a good way to get the feathers off if the goose must be cleaned in the field or a temporary camp. Slit the skin and pull it off.

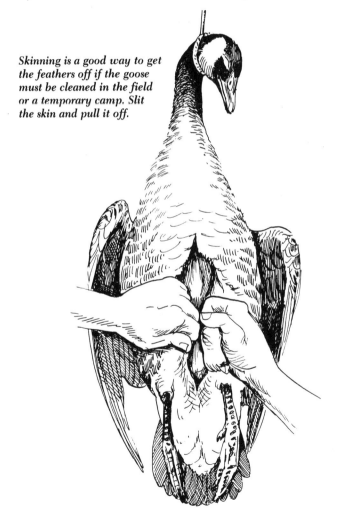

To skin a goose, follow the instructions on page 74, slitting the bird up the breast from tail to neck and stripping the skin and feathers away with pliers or your fingers. Then turn the goose over and slit it up the middle of the back and out the wings to the last joint. Cut off the wing at the last joint. Strip the skin off the back and wings; you will probably have to clip the flight feathers and cut off the tail bulb.

Cut off the head and wash the bird thoroughly, checking the flesh for pellets.

Sever the wings at the last joint, or simply cut them off next to the body; not much meat will go to waste.

Grouse

Range. The ruffed grouse is one of the most widely distributed game birds. There are ten recognized subspecies, and one or another is found almost every place in the United States, including Alaska, and in Canada, wherever extensive forest provides a habitat.

Ruffed grouse populations fluctuate widely. Over ten years the population increases, but within a year or two it falls to a fraction of the peak numbers. Then the cycle begins again.

Size. The ruffed grouse is a chickenlike bird about 18 inches long with a 22½-inch wingspan. The male weighs about 20 ounces; the female, about 19. But one grouse, bagged in the Adirondacks in New York, tipped the scales at 36 ounces.

Plumage. A ruff of feathers around the neck and a partial crest on the head distinguish the ruffed grouse. Its general coloration is light brown; the underparts are lighter. The bird is mottled with darker bars, darts, and arrow points. The ruff is usually jet black but may be iridescent with purples and metallic greens.

The male and female are a bit difficult to tell apart. In the male the black tail band is usually continuous, but in the female it is broken at the center by two unbanded feathers. Some females have an unbroken tail band, however, so experienced hunters measure the two center tail feathers: feathers longer than 5¼ inches almost always indicate a male, since the female grouse has shorter tail feathers.

For confirmation, dress the bird and examine the area of the backbone just behind the rib cage. The male's testes resemble two small, gray peas; the female egg sac is orange.

The ruffed grouse has 6-inch legs and three-toed feet. In winter the toes grow scaly fringes that act like snowshoes to keep the bird from sinking in the snow. The grouse is among the few birds to have feathers growing down its legs and covering the shank.

Behavior. Although the grouse can fly about 40 miles per hour for a short distance, it probably cannot fly more than a mile in sustained flight. It makes a loud, thundering noise when flushed, but if it is not startled into flight, it can also take off quietly. The bird has quick reflexes and can fly at top speed through thick forest, avoiding tree trunks and limbs with lightning shifts of direction.

Food. The ruffed grouse eats more than 600 varieties of plant and tree leaves, as well as fruit and insects. In winter, especially where snow covers the ground, tree buds make up most of the diet. Because of their large size, the buds of the male aspen are the most favored winter food. Some researchers believe the availability of this bud makes the difference between high and low grouse populations the next spring, since it determines how healthy the females are when they lay their eggs.

Reproduction. Grouse usually mate in May. The hen lays about twelve eggs and sits on them for twenty-four days until they hatch. All the eggs hatch the same day, usually in early June. Within a day the mother takes her chicks and leaves the nest, never to return. The chicks eat a diet of insects and fruit and in a few weeks can fly short distances.

The grouse brood stays together until early autumn, when most of the young disperse. They move out in all directions, some going only a few hundred yards, others many miles. In their search for territories of their own, grouse sometimes crash through windows and fly into cities. The area vacated by one grouse brood will likely be filled by other young grouse from other areas, and thus the total population in a patch of cover remains about the same.

Bobwhite

Range. The bobwhite quail ranges from southern Wisconsin east to the Atlantic, west to South Dakota, and south to the Gulf Coast of Mexico. More than twenty subspecies are distributed across its range. Bobwhite populations are low at present because of diminished habitat. Although the Southeast used to be the king of bobwhite country, Oklahoma, Texas, Iowa, Indiana, Delaware, and New Jersey now vie with Florida and South Carolina for the best hunting. The bird is hunted in thirty-five states.

Size. The bobwhite is a chunky quail. The average bird weighs 6 to 7 ounces, measures 9 to 10½ inches, and has a wingspan of 14 or 15 inches.

Plumage. The male has a white chin and throat and a white stripe that sweeps from bill to eye and down to the base of the neck. This white streak is bordered by a dark streak that widens and blends into a brown bib on the chest. The dark hazel crown has a short crest. The back is scaled and mottled brown, the sides and flanks are chestnut with ragged black-and-white bars and white spots. The wings are brown and gray. The white belly has brown and black Vs and specks.

The female has similar coloration. To tell the sexes apart, look at the face. The male has a white face; the female's is yellow. First-year quail can be distinguished from the adults by the light brown tips of the primary wing feathers.

Food. Bobwhites feed early in the morning on clear days, but as the season gets colder they begin feeding later in the day, and by late December they usually feed only during the warmest hours, around noon. On warm days, with bright sunshine, they spend most of their time in a cool, shady section of their territory.

Although the bobwhite eats insects, seeds are its primary food.

Weedy herbs, ragweed, and lespedezas are preferred. Other foods include soybeans, sorghum, corn, partridge peas, cowpeas, trailing wild beans, wheat, sunflower seeds, smartweed, and beggarweed.

Reproduction. The bobwhite breeds in January or February in the South, but in most of its range, March is the month. Males court females in the covey by turning their heads to show off their white markings and dragging their wings on the ground. They may also rush at other males. Once paired, both male and female scrape out a small nest on the ground, concealing it with dead grass and lining it with leaves and grass.

The female lays thirteen or fourteen creamy white eggs. If the nest is destroyed early during the incubation period, she nests again. Incubation takes about twenty-three days, and the eggs usually hatch in June. In late summer the family group begins to drift apart.

The young bobwhites become more and more gregarious, mixing and traveling with other coveys and wandering away from their family coveys.

Bobwhites are susceptible to predation by cats, dogs, skunks, raccoons, foxes, and most other carnivores. Many do not survive long enough to mate once, and almost none see a third spring. In captivity, however, bobwhites have lived eight years.

Grouse and quail

Grouse and quail can be cleaned by the methods given for small game birds (snipe, woodcock, pigeon, and dove) or by the technique given below, all of which bypass picking. Some hunters, however, pick any game bird large enough to warrant the trouble, since the skin and the layer of fat just under the skin add considerably to the flavor of the meat.

Eviscerating. Whether you choose to pick or not, remove the intestines soon after the bird is shot so that body fluids will not contaminate the meat. Hold the bird belly up with the feet gripped in your fingers. Use the fingers of the other hand to grasp the point of the breast and pull hard enough to open the abdominal cavity; or cut a slit with a knife. Hook out the guts with the fingers and tear the large intestine loose from the vent.

The bird is now ready for picking or skinning.

Picking. Either dry picking or wet picking will work for grouse and quail. Follow the directions given on pages 71–73.

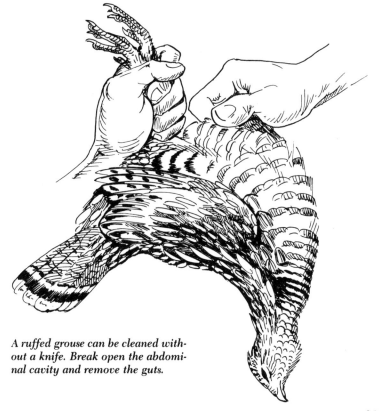

A ruffed grouse can be cleaned without a knife. Break open the abdominal cavity and remove the guts.

Skinning. As soon as possible after the bird is shot, while you are still in the field, pull off the head and twist off the wings. Starting at the breast, skin the bird by tearing the skin off. Leave the tail feathers attached if you want a trophy.

Once home, cut off the feet, cut out the vent, and cut off the tail bulb with its feathers still attached. Spread the feathers out and press them between boards until dry, then mount them for display.

Wash the carcass well to remove all impurities before cooking it.

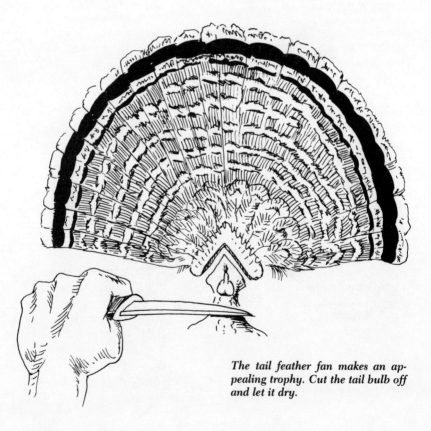

The tail feather fan makes an appealing trophy. Cut the tail bulb off and let it dry.

Pheasants
Ringneck

Range. The ring-necked pheasant is an import. The first successful planting was made at Corvallis, Oregon, in 1881, when twenty-one of these Chinese birds were released. In ten years they had stocked the entire Willamette Valley. Ringnecks had been released in ten other states by 1910.

Today ring-necked pheasants are found in Alberta and Saskatchewan, 400 miles north of the U.S. border. In the East the pheasant is found north of a line extending from the upper tip of the Chesapeake Bay to central Illinois. In the West pheasants are found north of a line from upper Missouri to southern Colorado to central California. Iowa, South Dakota, and Illinois are top pheasant-hunting states.

Current farming practices of leaving more land untilled are beneficial to pheasant nesting, and populations appear to be increasing over most of the bird's range.

Size. The rooster is about 3 feet long, including the 16- to 28-inch tail feathers, and weighs about 2½ to 3 pounds. Hens are smaller.

Plumage. The rooster's body is a spectacular blend of brown, copper, and russet sprinkled with black and white. There is a patch of light feathers on the rump, and the wings are light brown. The most noticeable markings on the cock are the white ring around its neck and the long tail feathers. These feathers are important to the pheasant: hens will not mate a rooster whose tail feathers are short. The rooster has a spur on the back of each leg that grows longer and sharper as he matures.

The hen is more subdued, mostly brown with a sprinkling of black-and-white feathers.

Food. Pheasants find food in cultivated fields, eating corn, soybeans, oats, wheat, and other seeds. Wild food includes berries, grapes, sumac, acorns, and alder buds. Pheasants also consume animal protein — insects, snails, and slugs. When pheasants can find unharvested fields, corn makes up about four-fifths of their diet.

Habitat. Pheasants inhabit grain fields until the harvest, then seek cover in weedy ditches, cattail marshes, weed patches, thick fencerows, even thick woods. Those birds that survive the winter usually were lucky enough to have found cover that provided both shelter and food.

Reproduction. Each dominant rooster may mate with six to eight hens. The hen builds a shallow nest in high, dead grass or grain stubble. She chooses a site that offers a ready supply of insects for the young birds when they hatch. The hen usually lays about a dozen eggs and broods them for about twenty-three days before they hatch.

The chicks can leave the nest almost as soon as they hatch. They follow the hen around in a group, scurrying rapidly and eating insects and plant material. The chicks can fly when they are about two weeks old, but the brood stays together until late summer.

Pheasant chicks are highly susceptible to predation. Dogs, cats, skunks, squirrels, foxes, coyotes, weasels, hawks, and owls catch about three-fourths of the chicks before October. Hunting season accounts for most of the remaining roosters, and the survivors must face winter winds, deep snow, short food supplies, and more hungry predators. The rooster's average lifespan is only about ten months, but the hen usually survives to twenty months.

Ringneck

A pheasant can be skinned very quickly, but most hunters pick this bird because the skin makes the carcass look and taste better.

Dressing. Open the pheasant and remove the intestines soon after it has been shot. Keep the liver, heart, and gizzard.

Remove the feathers, by either dry or wet picking. The sooner dry picking is done, the easier it will be. Pheasants can also be skinned.

Preparing the carcass. A pheasant may be roasted whole or cut into pieces for cooking. To section the bird, lay it on its back. Using a sharp knife, cut the legs off at the hip joint. Grasp the leg and push it away from the body. Slice through the skin and ligaments where the leg joins the body. If the cut is accurate, you can separate the leg

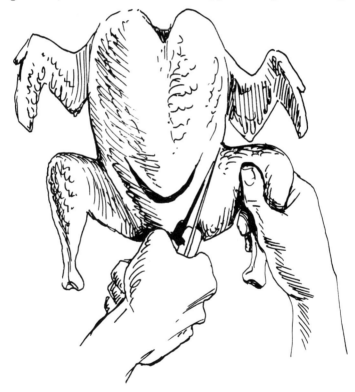

As you push the leg away from the body, the hip joint will become apparent; cut through to free the leg.

from the body at the hip joint without having to cut through bone. Usually, the drumstick and thigh are left intact.

Slice out the breast and wings with a boning knife. Leave each wing connected to each breast half; the breast sections can be cut into two pieces if they are too large for serving.

Pheasant breast is among the best of wild game dishes, so be sure not to leave any meat on the carcass.

Small birds
Snipe

Range. The common snipe (also called Wilson's snipe and jack-snipe) ranges across Alaska and most of Canada, south to California and Colorado in the West and to Pennsylvania and New Jersey in the East.

Snipe populations are sufficiently stable and plentiful to allow hunting in many states. They are difficult to flush from their boggy habitats and even harder to hit.

Size. The snipe is 10 inches long, with a long, slender, flesh-colored bill. It weighs about 7 ounces.

Plumage. The head, neck, and upper breast are buff streaked with brown. Brownish black stripes run from the bill up over the crown and down to the nape. The back and sides are a mixture of black, chestnut, and buff with white lateral streaks. The wings blend reddish brown, black, and white. The underbelly is white with brown streaks at the flank. The tail is wide and short, tipped with white and having a black subterminal band.

The snipe is sometimes confused with the woodcock, especially since it is found in the same habitat. But the legs distinguish the two birds. The woodcock has short, dark legs; the snipe has long, greenish legs.

Habitat. These birds live in remote, open bogs, flooded grassy meadows, and grassy patches along streams and lakes. When they are in their wintering grounds, where moist grassland is scarce, they congregate in alders, birches, and young maples, usually near water.

Snipes are not flocking birds, but during migration they travel in loose groups, often congregating in choice cover. They start migrating in September at the first frost and move slowly ahead of the advancing cold weather, usually flying at night. Some do not arrive in the South until December. The northward trek starts in March.

Food. The snipe finds food in damp soil, probing with its bill for beetles, other ground insects, insect larvae, and snails. It also takes grasshoppers, locusts, and a variety of plant-eating insects. The diet includes vegetation as well — smartweed, bullrush, panic grass, and other marsh plants.

The snipe dislikes bright light and heat and usually feeds in late afternoon.

Reproduction. The snipe breeds in May in northern regions and as early as mid-April in warmer areas. The male circles and dives and puts on an aerial display to attract the female. After they mate, she builds a shallow, grass-lined nest on a hummock in a boggy meadow or wetland. Her four olive-gray eggs are speckled and streaked with black markings. The eggs are incubated for twenty days.

The young are led away from the nest as soon as they have all hatched. The mother broods the chicks in bad weather and at night for their first few days. She feeds them earthworms and soft insects, but after several days they begin finding food on their own. They can fly when two weeks old and are well feathered by three weeks. Although able to care for themselves at four weeks, they often remain together as a family until fall.

Woodcock

Range. The woodcock is found east of the Plains to the Atlantic, from Manitoba to east Texas. At present, woodcock populations are highest in the upper Midwest and lowest in the Atlantic regions. However, populations appear to be increasing throughout most of the range.

Size. A woodcock is a stubby, 8-inch bird with short wings. It has a long bill — 2½ inches long in the male but 2¾ inches in the female. This is the quickest way to tell the sexes apart. The male woodcock weighs about 5½ ounces; the female is heavier, weighing 7 ounces.

Plumage. The head is buff with a black line from bill to eye. The bird has a small black ear covert patch and wide black crossbars on the back of the head and the nape.

The general body coloration is mottled brown. The breast is cinnamon, the underparts buff, and the back, rump, and scapulars mottled black, gray, brown, and reddish yellow. The tail has black-and-white tips; the primaries are dusky gray. The bird's color scheme is almost perfect camouflage.

Habitat. The woodcock's favorite vegetation is alder shrubs. Under alders, ground cover is usually sparse, earthworms are plentiful, and the soil is moist — ideal conditions for woodcock feeding. The bird also feeds at the edges of ponds and puddles but usually emerges into open areas only at night.

Woodcocks have few natural enemies. Their population is regulated by the availability of cover for feeding and nesting.

Food. The woodcock eats its weight in food nearly every day. Earthworms constitute about 85 percent of the diet. Excellent night vision enables the bird to hunt mostly at night, when earthworms are on top of the ground or active in their underground tunnels. It has sensitive ears to hear the worms, and it may feel their vibrations.

When it detects a worm underground, it inserts its long beak into the soil. The upper beak is prehensile and can be wrapped around the worm's body to lift it out of the ground. The woodcock leaves a nail-sized hole in the ground called a boring. These holes and large splashes of white feces, often called chalk, are good evidence that woodcocks are about.

Reproduction. The woodcock migrates north early in the spring. The male arrives first, sometimes even before the snow melts, and begins singing to attract a mate.

After mating, the female builds a nest, usually on a well-drained rise in thick cover. Her four eggs hatch in twenty-eight days. She broods the chicks for two weeks, and although young woodcocks are mature in four weeks, they often stay together as a family until the first frost, when they begin the migration south.

Although woodcocks do not fly in flocks, large numbers move simultaneously through the same cover, creating remarkable congregations in some areas. Following rivers and streams, they fly from alder patch to alder patch on their unhurried migration to the Louisiana wintering grounds.

Bandtail

Range. Band-tailed pigeons breed in the far western mountains ranges from southwestern British Columbia into Mexico. Researchers do not know their total number because they are migratory and live in remote regions. Moreover, their numbers vary considerably from year to year. But 250,000 pigeons were once observed in Kern County, California, and several other counties have also reported large flocks, especially during the winter migration. No doubt a huntable population exists all across its range.

Size. The band-tailed pigeon resembles the city pigeon in size and form. It is large and husky, about 15 inches long, weighing up to a pound but averaging 11 to 12 ounces. The female is slightly smaller than the male.

Plumage. The head, neck, and underparts of the male are purplish brown fading to off-white on the lower belly. A narrow white crescent makes a half collar on the nape of the neck. Below it is a patch of iridescent bronze and green feathers. The back is dark greenish brown, fading into bluish gray on the rump and tail. A wide black band crosses the midtail, and the tip of the tail is pale bluish gray. The wing quill feathers are dark; the wing coverts are a dark bluish gray with light gray edgings. The bill is yellow with a black tip, and the eyelids are red and naked.

In the female the iridescent patch on the neck is less pronounced, and the white collar is less prominent.

Food. The favorite food of band-tailed pigeons is acorns, and if the supply is good, they live almost entirely on these nutritious nuts. They also eat seeds and fruits, plus some grasshoppers and other large insects. Barley, wheat, oats, cherries, grapes, walnuts, and peas are some favored cultivated crops.

Habitat. The band-tailed pigeon favors natural forests, high

101

altitudes, and rugged terrain. In spring it looks for mountain slopes covered with conifers and hardwoods. When the nesting duties are done, the bandtail usually flies to lower altitudes to feed, returning to the mountains in the evening to roost.

Reproduction. Bandtails fly to the southern part of their range in October or November and start migrating north again in January or February. Some move only a few miles into mountains to nest; others fly as far north as Washington and British Columbia. They pair off as soon as they arrive in the nesting rounds if they don't already have mates.

The male pigeon selects a territory for nesting and attracts the female by sitting on a prominent perch and cooing loudly. He stretches his neck down, opens the bill slightly, and gathers in air to fill the neck skin to three times its natural size. While the neck is inflated, he calls, then deflates. The call sounds like that of a small owl.

The pigeons may not nest at once, but when they do, they select a territory that has forest cover and also a nearby source of water. The female may take a week or more to build the nest—a haphazard structure.

The female lays a single, pure white egg, rarely two eggs. Incubation takes eighteen to twenty days, and both male and female participate. Weather seems to affect the incubation period, probably because air can penetrate the nest from the bottom.

The young pigeon emerges naked from the egg. It eats "pigeon milk" regurgitated from glands in the crops of both parents, both of whom help in brooding. At first it is fed three times a day; later, only twice daily. The "milk" begins to contain more and more vegetable material. Finally, the young pigeon is fed mostly seeds and fruit, and the parents spend more time away from the nest. At about thirty days the pigeon is on its own and can fly away.

Dove

Range. The mourning dove has the largest range of our game birds — the forty-eight contiguous states, central Mexico, Cuba, Haiti, and Canada from British Columbia to Ontario. In winter most mourning doves are found south of a line from California to New Jersey.

There are two subspecies of mourning doves, with the Great Plains dividing the western variety from the eastern. Populations of both are high and currently stable.

Size. This sleek, streamlined bird is about 12 inches long, with a 17- to 19-inch wingspread. It weighs about 4 ounces. The female is slightly smaller than the male, with a shorter tail.

Plumage. The male mourning dove has a grayish brown back and rump. The lateral tail feathers are bluish gray with a black crossbar and a white tip. The outer tail feathers are white on the web as well. The neck and head are fawn with a bluish gray crown and a patch of bare skin around the eye. The lower sides of the neck are iridescent purple, bronze, and gold. There is a small, glossy, bluish black spot beneath the ear coverts. The flight feathers show some bluish gray.

The dove's underparts are buff with a purplish cast. The breast is darkest; the throat, chin, and under-the-tail coverts are paler. The flanks are bluish gray.

The female's coloration is not so bright as the male's.

Food. Mourning doves are almost wholly seed eaters. They consume corn, wheat, oats, and the other cultivated grains. Legumes, like soybeans and peanuts, and the leaves of most green plants are also eaten, as are hollyberries, seeds from pinecones, and most weed seeds.

Reproduction. Although doves nesting in the southern states may breed in January and February, the birds that fly north for nesting usually start the mating rituals in March or April.

The male selects a territory and defends it against other males. He attracts females by sitting in a prominent place, such as a dead branch, electric wire, or farm fence, and cooing — an activity that excludes nearly everything else, since he coos from dawn to dusk. After a female is selected, the pair find a nesting site and the male performs his spectacular nuptial flight. He coos loudly several times, then leaps from his perch and flies in a steep climb, often attaining a height of 150 feet. Then he sets his wings, spreads his tail feathers, and glides in a large spiral back to the female.

After mating, the male brings sticks to the female, who constructs a loose platform. She lays her first egg soon after the nest is built; her second egg appears a few days later. She immediately starts brooding.

Both male and female incubate the eggs, which hatch in about fourteen days. Doves feed their young by regurgitating food. The young birds grow rapidly and often leave the nest in about two weeks. Soon after they have left, the parents start nesting again. They may hatch three to five broods, depending on how far south they are nesting.

Small birds

Snipe, woodcock, pigeon, and dove can be cleaned by dry or wet picking the feathers. If the feathers cannot be picked immediately and the weather is warm, eviscerate the bird and place the carcass in the shade or in an ice chest as soon as possible.

To get the bird ready for table quickly without picking it, use one of the following methods.

Breast only, without a knife. This method is well adapted to preparing a dove. Hold the bird in one hand, breast up. With your other hand, feel for the point of the breast, grasp it, and pull upward. The breast and wings will break loose from the carcass.

Twist off the wings. Pull any breast skin that remains. The bird is now ready to be washed.

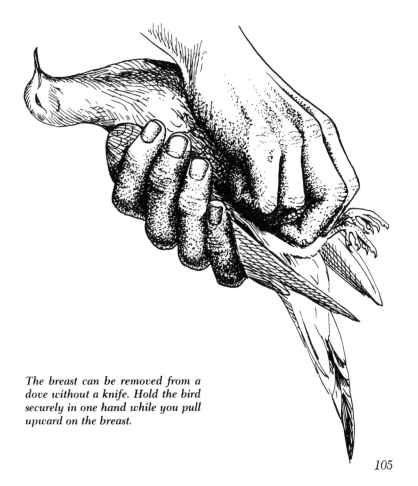

The breast can be removed from a dove without a knife. Hold the bird securely in one hand while you pull upward on the breast.

Breast only, with a knife. Eviscerate the bird by slitting the abdomen under the point of the breast and pulling the guts out. Now there is no danger of puncturing the innards as you perform the next step.

Using a knife, cut around the breast and lift it out. Peel off the skin with its feathers and wash the flesh.

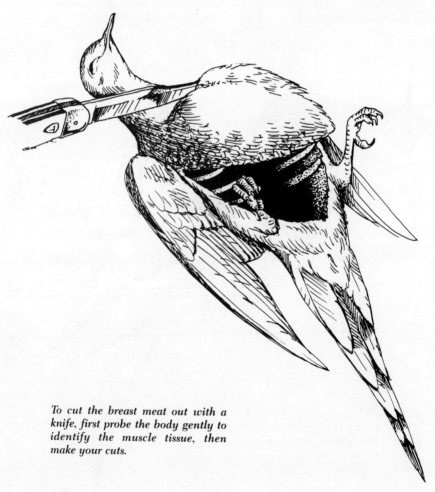

To cut the breast meat out with a knife, first probe the body gently to identify the muscle tissue, then make your cuts.

Legs, too. Soon after shooting the bird, cut off the head, wings, and legs with a sharp knife. Remove the legs at the first joint instead of at the hip.

To remove the guts, pluck the feathers from around the vent and make a slit from the vent forward. Reach inside and pull out the intestines.

Strip the skin and feathers off the carcass. Once washed, it is ready to cook.

Although a woodcock's legs are barely worth a nibble, you may find the carcass more appetizing if they are left on.

Breast meat in two pieces. With this method there is no need to eviscerate, disjoint, or pick the bird. Simply fillet out the breast meat by slicing down to the breast-bone on each side of the cartilage. Turn the knife at a 90-degree angle and remove the breast meat in two sections, then peel off the skin with its feathers.

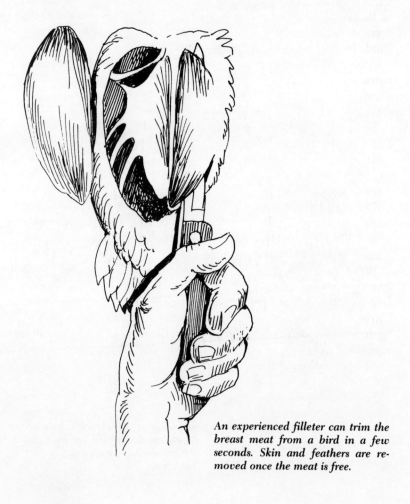

An experienced filleter can trim the breast meat from a bird in a few seconds. Skin and feathers are removed once the meat is free.

Turkeys

Range. When the Jamestown colony was formed, wild turkeys were found all across the United States. But extensive hunting and land clearing cut their numbers, until in 1940 only nineteen states still had turkeys. Since then, better management practices and extensive restocking have helped the wild turkey regain most of its former territory, and by 1985 thirty-five states had huntable populations.

Size. There are five subspecies of turkeys — the Eastern, Florida, Rio Grande, Merriam's, and Goulds. The Eastern and Merriam's are the largest. An Eastern gobbler is about 36 inches long, including its tail, stands 15 inches high, and weighs 15 to 20 pounds. The hens are smaller and weigh 9 to 12 pounds.

Plumage. The wild gobbler has bronze body feathers that darken to almost black on its back. The wings are barred white and dark brown, and the tail has brown-and-black bars. The long legs are reddish, with long, sharp spurs.

From the gobbler's chest projects a beard that looks and feels like hog bristles; it grows 8 or 9 inches. The gobbler's head is naked. Wattles hang from the chin and throat, and the lower throat and neck are knotty with fatty growths called caruncles. A fleshy snood hangs over his bill. His face is covered with pale blue skin, but when he is excited, the skin turns blood red.

The turkey hens are less flamboyant in their coloration than the gobblers.

Food. Turkeys are mostly vegetarians, but insects are important food for the young poults, and adults eat insects when they are available. Other foods include chufa grass, sumac, wild grapes, ragweed, most berries, corn, wheat, sorghum, and oats. The birds feed extensively on acorns, beechnuts, hazelnuts, and conifer seeds, depending on their availability. Turkeys usually feed just after dawn and just before dark.

Habitat. Turkeys must have tall trees to roost in, thick cover for hiding and nesting, and a reliable source of water. Most mammalian predators prey on turkeys, and owls catch them after dark. A mature turkey is fairly safe from predators, however, because it is large and wary.

Reproduction. Turkeys start their mating ritual in April in the North and February or March in the South. The gobblers separate from the bachelor groups in which they have passed the winter and call loudly to attract hens.

The hen flocks break up into groups of three or four per gobbler. Each hen tamps a shallow nest in the grass or leaves. The gobbler mates with her several times during the egg-laying process. She incubates her ten to twelve eggs for about four weeks while he guards his harem against other gobblers. Sometimes the males confront each other in fights, which characteristically are more noise and bluff than battle.

The poults stay with their mother until the following spring. In the fall the females join with other family groups or unmated hens to form a winter flock. The males find their places in bachelor groups, which are often segregated by age, with the flocks of older gobblers usually the smallest.

Turkey

Dressing a turkey is more difficult than dressing a pheasant or a grouse, but you have a choice of ways to do it. And the dinner will be worth the effort. The heart, liver, and gizzard are delicious eating, so be sure to save them.

Bleeding. Some hunters bleed the turkey first because they believe it improves the flavor of the meat. Make a slit across the throat, just in front of the breast, and hang the bird so that the blood drips out.

Eviscerating. Remove the innards as soon as possible. Make a slit from the vent to the point of the breast and pull out the entrails, cutting tissue where necessary. The operation is easier if you first pull the feathers from this area.

A gobbler is an exciting bird to bring down. Your hands may still be shaking, but eviscerate the bird right away. Pluck the feathers from the abdomen, then make the slit.

Picking. Turkeys can be dry picked or wet picked. If you have time to pick the bird right after it is shot, dry picking will be easy. After a few hours, when the bird has cooled off and the feathers have set, wet picking will be easier.

Skinning. Turkeys can also be skinned. Cut off the head and snip the wings at the last joint. Using the point of the knife, cut the skin up the breast, from vent to neck, and down the back, from neck to tail. Peel off the skin. If the flight feathers on the wings do not come off, clip them with shears.

Preparing the carcass. Wash the picked or skinned turkey and roast it whole or cut it into pieces. Turkey legs are removed from the body at the hip joint, the wings at the first joint. Cut out the backbone and split the breast; you may need a meat saw to cut it in half.

The meat can also be removed from the bones. Using a filleting or boning knife, bone out the breast according to the instructions given for bluebills on pages 81–82, and then bone the wings and legs. Reserve all the bones for making soup.

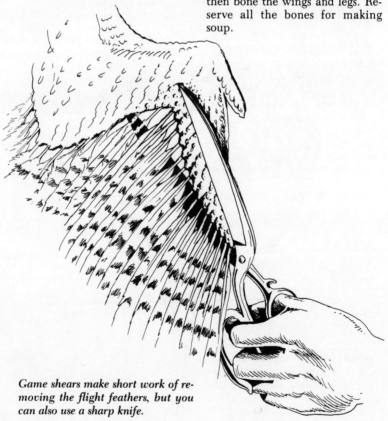

Game shears make short work of re-moving the flight feathers, but you can also use a sharp knife.